ET   30063

S0-BID-906

ATHLETICS FOR STUDENT AND COACH

Athletics

For Student and Coach

NEW, REVISED EDITION

IAN WARD & DENIS WATTS

PELHAM BOOKS

0829799 ~~650063~~

First published in Great Britain by
PELHAM BOOKS LTD
52 Bedford Square
London, W.C.1
AUGUST 1967
SECOND IMPRESSION JANUARY 1969
THIRD IMPRESSION MAY 1970
FOURTH IMPRESSION OCTOBER 1971
SECOND EDITION 1976

© *1967 by Ian Ward and Denis Watts*

*All Rights Reserved. No part of this publication
may be reproduced, stored in a retrieval system,
or transmitted, in any form or by any means, elec-
tronic, mechanical, photocopying, recording or
otherwise, without the prior permission of the
Copyright owner.*

ISBN 0 7207 0881 8

*Printed lithographically in Great Britain by Hollen Street
Press Ltd. at Slough and bound by James Burn at Esher,
Surrey.*

Dedicated to

OBADIAH SMEW

who so clearly indicated the heights
to which the uncoached athlete could
aspire, if not achieve

ACKNOWLEDGEMENTS

All photographs related to fitness training are by P. Davies and A. Godsmark.

All sketches are by Carol Powell of Madeley College.

Jumping 'Decathlon' Tables by Wilf Paish – permission given by *Athletics Coach*, published by the Amateur Athletic Association.

Assistance with Race Walking – Harold Whitlock.

High jump (Fosbury) sequence by A. S. Kennard.

Sequence of B. Kannenberg Race Walking by Tissot van Patot.

CONTENTS

9

030663

0829799

10 *Contents*

ILLUSTRATIONS

Introduction

This book is written primarily for the club coach and the student in College or University. It is based on the authors' experiences of working with athletes from club through to international level, and deals with the practical problems of coaching.

It is assumed that the reader possesses reasonable background knowledge of athletics and that he wishes to further this knowledge and apply it in the coaching situation. This book presents the basics of coaching. The book is not exhaustive and does not deal with advanced details of athletic techniques: it selects, from the wealth of technical information available, those aspects which are of greatest importance to the coach. In terms of technique, an attempt has been made to answer the following questions:

Which features of the event are of the greatest importance?
Where should the coach stand and what should he look for?
What are the major faults likely to be seen in an event?
What should the coach say to the athlete in order to help him to correct these major faults?

The book also suggests how the coach can help the athlete in the planning of training schedules, in the 'balancing-out' of speed, strength, stamina and skill training at various times of the year.

An attempt has been made to set coaching in perspective with regard to the sport of athletics and to education, and to provide a basis for the coaching of the young athlete. The authors also realise that there are many athletes who cannot obtain the help of a coach. It is hoped that these athletes may find something of value in this book.

This revised edition incorporates generally accepted changes in technique; in particular the 'Fosbury' high jump technique is added. Event distances and training sessions are generally discussed in metric terms although the generally accepted imperial terms are used for some measurements.

DENIS WATTS   IAN WARD

1 The Place of Coaching in Athletics

Teaching

When we refer to the teaching of athletics we are mainly concerned with the introduction of an event to a group of youngsters. We generally think of the school situation in which the master in charge of P.E. plans a syllabus of athletics for all the youngsters in the school, with teaching taking place during the school time-table. This initial work is usually somewhat formal in nature. This is because of the large number of youngsters involved and because of safety precautions. The aim in this work is to transmit basic knowledge to all youngsters, coupled with an understanding and appreciation of athletics.

Coaching

Coaching follows teaching. The large group situation breaks down to small groups and perhaps eventually to individuals. In effect, teaching is for the group and coaching is for the keener individuals – but we must bear in mind that these individuals will often work as a keen group. Coaching implies a small number of athletes, and is the follow-up to the teaching situation. Yet this does not put it outside the school situation. Whilst the teacher's main aim is to interest a large number of youngsters in athletics, he accepts that some will be much keener than others. The teacher's time for the basic teaching of athletics will be limited – for athletics is no more important than any other school sport – but keen youngsters will wish to follow up the sport. This may be done partly within school time and partly on the basis of the school athletics club with the teacher working with youngsters on an individual basis. This will almost invariably involve one or two club sessions a week outside school time – usually from 4.00–5.00 p.m. This now represents the situation in which we would say that the schoolmaster is coaching his squad of young athletes. Often this coaching is little more than *advising* – but it represents an essentially voluntary relationship which places it slightly outside the teacher-pupil situation that pertains in normal classes.

Coaching at the level of club athletics represents quite another relationship. In the school the enthusiastic teacher can sell almost any sport and see it flourish – one of the reasons being that he limits the choice. He may establish the pattern of 'peer sports' within the school. Attitudes and skills learnt in the school will obviously influence (for *and* against) the sports that are to be followed at the end of one's school career. The wise teacher relates his school work to the practices of the community (but he may occasionally lead the community to fresh sports) and ensures that youngsters from the school move easily into the adult sporting world. He does not merely tell them that there is a town athletics club: he *takes* them to the club, introduces them to the secretary and coach. He should also spend some time at the club himself. He perhaps uses an occasional club official as a helper at school meets and on the school Sports Day, and arranges fixtures for his older boys against the club's Youths or Juniors.

The teacher might also promote one or two Senior Invitation events in connection with the School Sports. Certainly he should at all times work for close connections with the local club and ensure that the youngster's transition from school athletics to club athletics is a smooth transition.

In athletics there are a number of athletes who have achieved excellence without the aid of a coach, and it is good for this to happen, for the coach must never be seen as a panacea! However, those athletes who have succeeded without the obvious help of a coach have generally been athletes in the non-technical events of middle distance and long distance running. When athletes succeed in the technical events without the direct aid of a coach, they have almost always been intelligent, well-read athletes who have learnt much from other athletes and from athletics literature. In effect they are self-coached, gleaning information from a variety of sources and evaluating that information before applying it to their training. If their evaluation is sound, then they become successful, independent athletes to be much admired. But if their evaluation is unsound they fail, and the coaches see good physical material never fulfilling its potential. In all cases the athlete is advised to seek the aid of a club coach. When he cannot find the help that he needs, *then* he must face up to the problem of self-coaching.

At club level the coach must accept the freedom of the athlete to reject him. Some athletes do not wish to be coached, preferring to sort out their own problems. Other athletes do not wish to bring the seriousness of coaching into their athletics, for their interests may be recreative and social rather than competitive. What the coach should try to do is to place himself in a position to help a number of athletes by virtue of his knowledge, manner and availability. Thereafter, with no ill-will, there is the possibility of the coach deciding whether or not to help an athlete on a long term basis. The athlete also needs to take the decision of accepting or rejecting the offer of help. In the majority of cases the club coach will help, in varying degrees, the majority of club members. If the club is large then it is probable that there will be more than one coach and that the coaching load will be shared. In all clubs, however, there may be athletes who prefer to pursue their training without any reference to the coach. This is a situation which should be accepted amicably by all club members.

2. The Fundamentals of Coaching

Athletics as a sport is based on the individual athlete. On rare occasions there are officials who have become far removed from the club athlete, and who may give the impression that athletics is for the officials. On rarer occasions there are coaches who feel that athletics revolves round them, that their 'squad' represents the 'in-group', and that they must appear to be connected with everything in athletics that is successful. This is vanity, and the vain coach puts 'self' before the sport and the athletes. We must face up to the reality of coaching, which is that coaches in Britain are not accepted as being very important, and that coaches in this country have little authority. Basically they are the servants of the athletes, giving time and knowledge to the athletes and gaining satisfaction in return.

To be in a position to coach effectively, we must consider the needs of the athlete.

From the coach, the athlete needs
   (a) Sound advice and guidance
   (b) Regular and sympathetic coaching
   (c) Encouragement and inspiration.

Fundamentals of Coaching
The first need of the coach is the availability of time. You *may* be a Senior Coach with excellent technical knowledge. Your knowledge is of no value to the athlete unless you are prepared to make it available at the track. The coach needs to have the time and to be willing to attend the track regularly. The athlete needs to know that the coach will be at

18

the track, on the same evening and at the same time, for at least 40 weeks of the year. Twice a week might be better from the point of view of a club. The athlete needs to know that the coach will welcome him, guide him, bully him if necessary – but that the coach will always be there. Herein lies a fine difference between coaching and advising. The club coach may not be guide and mentor to all athletes at the club – but he fulfils a useful role simply by virtue of a regular and pleasant presence. If he welcomes all athletes to the track then he is doing good work for his club. If he can offer sound advice then he is doing even better work. And if he is also coaching some of the athletes (and this involves a much greater degree of involvement) then he is well on the way to helping build a successful club. In effect, the coach *coaches* the athletes that he wants to coach. However the sympathetic coach is also prepared to offer *advice* to any athlete who is prepared to make the effort to walk across the track and ask for it.

A second fundamental of coaching is the ability to establish a happy relationship with individual athletes. Technical knowledge alone is not enough, and the coach's manner must be such that athletes are happy to approach him, converse with him and respect his advice. The coach for his part must accept that the aims of the athlete are essentially selfish.

The task of the coach is to help the athlete to achieve excellence, and in order to do this the coach must initially consider the needs of the athlete. If the coach decides that he is prepared to help an athlete on a regular basis then he must define his responsibilities to the athlete. Then he must say to himself 'Can we establish a working relationship?' If the relationship lacks sympathy, then there is little chance of a successful partnership. The coach should say this, and should then try to arrange for the athlete to be coached by someone else. If this is not possible then the coach should make himself available for occasional advice. The coach who is prepared to help an athlete also needs to define and state the athlete's responsibilities to the coach.

The coach also needs the ability to inspire *realistically*. This must be an inspiration based on knowledge of the potentialities of the athlete, and confidence in the athlete. There is no point inspiring an athlete into thinking that he can achieve a particular performance if that performance is well beyond his capabilities. The inspiration of the coach must be soundly based. Inspiration that leads to nothing is valueless. The coach working with a fresh group of athletes can often stir the athletes to fleeting excitement in order to sell himself, his subject or to flatter his own ego. But the coach who is continuing to work with an athlete must think of the immediate effect of his words, and of the long term effects. Confidence transmitted needs a sound base. Perhaps one of the most exciting things for a coach to say to an athlete is:

'Conditions permitting, on Saturday you will run faster than you have ever run before.'

But this is a statement that one can rarely make. We must inspire athletes to train effectively, and to produce excellence in selected competitions. But as lay-psychologists we must not let the tongue run beyond the reason.

Happy relationships do not, however, stop with the athlete. It is essential to establish a working relationship with the groundsman – and this may mean a lot of give and take. If the groundsman is getting the track ready for Saturday's big meet, then perhaps we need to keep our squad off that vital inside lane. The good groundsman likes to see his track used and in the best possible condition for the big meets: we should help him when we can. Occasionally our squad may lend the groundsman a hand – at rush times help is much appreciated, and in any case our athletics is almost certainly being subsidised. But this does not mean that we must be 'groundsman dominated'. In some cases it may be necessary to take a stand against the occasional groundsman who merely sees athletes as a nuisance. The good groundsman, like the good coach, is interested in athletes. He also likes to have his contribution to athletics appreciated.

The coach should also work to establish happy relationships with the club secretary and the club committee. Occasional problems may arise between coach and secretary or between coach and committee, particularly when there is a clash of interest between the plans of the coach for an individual athlete and the needs of the club team.

Differences of opinion, however, should not lead to bitter dispute. When differences of opinion occur both the officials and the coach should ask themselves:

'Is my present position affected by personal considerations?' Clubs cannot thrive on internal disputes, and the individual is rarely as important as the club. Both club administrators and club coaches must be mindful of the needs of the athlete and the needs of the club. Personal disputes rarely benefit the sport.

The coach also needs basic equipment. This begins with a reasonably smart track suit (not too old-fashioned!) and training shoes. The coach needs to look the part! The coach will also need a warm anorak, for he will be spending much of his time standing round ... but he must bear in mind that he should

FIG. 1. THE COACH

do some work with the athletes ... even though he may be well past his prime, basic fitness is appreciated by the athletes. When fitness is preached, it must be practised. Physical condition adds authority of presentation to the coach's knowledge and understanding. The athlete will not expect magnificent personal prowess from the coach, but he will appreciate evidence of the coach's belief in fitness.

Basic equipment should also include whistle, stop watch, tape measure and notebook. The coach may also use a recording board. (Fig. 1) The coach also needs to know the availability of First Aid, and it is useful for the coach to possess a First Aid Certificate.

Knowledge of athletics is an obvious fundamental of coaching. The coach needs to possess a general background of knowledge of the sport, and to be *au fait* with current happenings both at local and national level. The coach also needs specialist event knowledge. Whilst he may feel that he would like to coach all events, he will probably find that he is inclined towards an event or group of events. The young coach should plan initially for depth of knowledge in one field, noting parathentically that depth acquired in one field will eventually mean a spread of knowledge, and possibly a spread of coaching interests. The competent sprints coach might easily find that he is working with a youngster who is not quite good enough as a sprinter. The coach might then suggest a switch to long jump or triple jump or hurdles, and will then work to improve his own coaching ability in the selected event.

Having worked for depth of knowledge in one field, and having taken the B.A.A.B. Coaching Award in that event or events, the young coach should then study related events and take the appropriate awards. He should then move back to specialisation in greater depth in preparation for the B.A.A.B. Senior Award.

B.A.A.B. COACHES

(a) Each Joint Coaching Committee maintains a register of B.A.A.B. Club Coaches and Senior Coaches who have offered their services free to Clubs and Schools, although travelling and any other expenses should be offered to them.

Applications for the services of B.A.A.B. Coaches should be made through the Honorary Coaching Secretary of the appropriate Joint Coaching Committee. These will supply the names and addresses of B.A.A.B. Coaches where available. A stamped addressed envelope must be enclosed.

(b) Grouping of Events and Abbreviations.

Groups

100 Metres ⎫	Sprinting
200 Metres ⎬	Group
400 Metres ⎭	(Spts.)

800 Metres ⎫	Middle
1,500 Metres ⎬	Distance
5,000 Metres ⎭	Group

100 Metres Hurdles ⎫		
200 Metres Hurdles		(Women)
400 Metres Hurdles ⎰	Hurdles	
	Group	
110 Metres Hurdles	(Hds.)	
400 Metres Hurdles ⎭		(Men)

Track Events (Track)

Marathon	(Mar.)	Shot Putt	(SP)
Steeplechase	(SC)	Discus	(Discus)
Long Jump	(LJ)	Javelin	(Jav.)
High Jump	(HJ)	Hammer	(Ham.)
Triple Jump	(Tr.J.)	*Relay Racing	(RR)
Pole Vault	(PV)	Long Distance and	
		Cross-Country	(LDC)
		Race Walking	(RW)

(c) One of the aims of the Scheme is to have a large number of qualified B.A.A.B. Coaches throughout the country. It is through the work of these and the National Coaches that the general standard of Athletics can be improved.

Those wishing to take the examination for the B.A.A.B. Club Coach or B.A.A.B. Senior Coach awards should write to the Honorary Secretary of the appropriate Joint Committee who will provide application forms for completion, and give the necessary information regarding the date, venue and time of the examination.

090065

EXAMINATION FOR B.A.A.B. SENIOR COACH

Qualification

Ability to coach a senior athlete up to the highest standard.

Examination

To be held periodically in each Area/Region.

Type

Written and Practical.

(a) Written Test:

Procedure. Any one of the following groups may be taken at any one examination:

Sprinting Group

or Distance Running Group ⎫ 3-hour papers

or Hurdling Group

or

Any one of the following events (2½-hour papers).

Marathon, Relay Racing; Steeplechasing; Shot Putt; Discus; Javelin; Hammer; High Jump; Long Jump; Triple Jump; Pole Vault; Race Walking.

Note: An applicant must first pass the written test before he is eligible to take the practical.

The written test, once passed, need not be taken again.

Note: Written examinations will usually be held on the last Sunday in February and October, and at a central venue under Area arrangements.

(b) Practical Test:

The National Coaches will conduct the practical examinations. The applicant is tested on the track with one or two of his own athletes whom he is coaching as demonstrators. He is presented with a number of coaching situations and asked to deal with them. An applicant may be tested with loop films to see whether he has the required knowledge of technique and a 'coaching eye'.

Results. Results of both written and practical tests will be notified to all candidates and the appropriate Joint Coaching Committee by the B.A.A.B. Coaching Office.

Examination Fees. The fee to sit a written examination is £1.00 (covering both written and practical). A fee of £1.00 will be charged an applicant who has passed the written test but having failed the practical wishes to be re-examined after a period of six months has elapsed.

Eligibility to take Examination. The applicant must have reached the age of 21 years. He must either be a B.A.A.B. Club Coach of more than 2 years qualification, unless a National Coach specially recommends that this waiting time should be less, in the event(s) in which he is taking the Senior Examination, or, have represented Gt. Britain in a Full International in the event for which he applies. International Athletes who have represented Gt. Britain in a Full International may be excused the Written Examination for the event in which they represented Gt. Britain upon recommendation of a National Coach. All applicants must also provide evidence that they have had considerable coaching experience.

Applications. Candidates should apply to the Honorary Secretary of the appropriate Joint Coaching Committee who will provide application form for completion, and inform date, venue and time of written test.

Subject Matter of Examination.

    (i) Technique – based upon a knowledge of simple mechanical principle.

    (ii) Acquisition of skills – i.e. the process of building up and improving technique.

    (iii) Faults – their cause, detection and correction.

    (iv) Training principles, and exercises.

    (v) Tactics – where applicable.

    (vi) Rules of competition.

    (vii) History and development of the event(s) including recent performances.

Re-examination. Failed candidates may apply for re-examination at any time after six months from the date of their last attempt.

Badges. Candidates who are successful in qualifying as a B.A.A.B. Senior Coach may wear the appropriate B.A.A.B. Badge obtainable from the B.A.A.B. Coaching Office.

Definition. A B.A.A.B. Senior Coach is one who:

    (a) Will coach, as far as possible, anyone requesting to be coached.

    (b) If an Active Athlete, will not accept fees which would prejudice his or her Amateur status.

EXAMINATION FOR B.A.A.B. CLUB COACH

Qualification. Ability to coach athletes up to normal Club standard.

Examination. To be held periodically in each Area as and when required.

Examiners. Only a National Coach, or selected B.A.A.B. Senior Coach in the event(s) in which he is so qualified, may conduct this test.

Type. Practical and Oral. This test will take approximately 45 minutes. Candidates should, if possible, provide their own athletes.

Procedure. The following may be taken at any one examination: One group of events or one event from list of events. Only in exceptional circumstances will permission be given for more than one group of events or more than one event to be taken at any one time when a separate form for each event (or group of events) must be completed.

Results. Results of examination will be notified to all candidates by the appropriate Joint Coaching Committee.

Examination Fees. £1.00 per Group, or event. Fees to be submitted with application form.

Eligibility to take Examinations
   (a) Age Limit. Minimum Age 19 years.
   (b) Evidence of coaching experience is required.
   (c) Participation in a Residential or Non-residential coaching course is desirable.

Applications. Candidates should apply to the Honorary Secretary of the appropriate Joint Coaching Committee who will provide application form for completion and inform date, venue and time of test.

Subject Matter of Examination. The applicant will be examined in:
   (a) His method of coaching the event(s);
   (b) His knowledge of the technique of the event(s) and, where applicable, the method of building up the technique;
   (c) Training for the event(s), including limbering up and exercises;
   (d) The tactics of the event(s) where applicable;
   (e) The rules of Competition for the event(s).

Re-examination. Failed candidates may apply for re-examination at any time after six months from the date of their last attempt.

Badges. Candidates who are successful in qualifying as a B.A.A.B. Club Coach may wear the appropriate B.A.A.B. Badge obtainable from the B.A.A.B. Coaching Office.

Definition. A B.A.A.B. Club Coach is one who:

(a) Will coach, as far as possible, anyone requesting to be coached.

(b) If an Active Athlete, will not accept fees which would prejudice his or her Amateur status.

The coach's knowledge is not always greater than that of the athlete. During the initial stages of a coaching relationship the coach will almost certainly know more than the athlete. As the coaching relationship progresses, however, the athlete's knowledge will increase at a greater rate than that of the coach because the coach is continually feeding relevant information to the athlete. This does not mean to say that the coach can no longer help the athlete; it means that the function of the coach changes as the athlete grows in stature. The coach can still help the athlete because he will have learnt what is of importance to this particular athlete. He *knows* the athlete. His help is of less importance than it was in earlier years, for he will have partially succeeded in his aim, which is to help the athlete to help himself. The great coach eventually fades into the background, leaving a successful and independent athlete.

The good coach constantly seeks to increase his knowledge. He should be familiar with the B.A.A.B. Instructional Booklets and with magazines relating to athletics. He should read through relevant books, bearing in mind that books should be read critically and not followed blindly. He should check appropriate articles in P.E. magazines, and should study loop films.

The coach's best source of knowledge is the track – here he will observe, talk, question athletes, listen to other coaches, experiment, observe the effects of his suggestions. Basically coaching is learnt at the track, and the coach is always learning. Probably the best way to learn how to coach an event is to find a talented youngster of about 16 years of age and coach him for some 3 to 4 years. Having done this it probably means that the thoughtful coach can coach this youngster, and that he is well on the way to being able to coach the *event:* but from the next athlete in this event, the coach will learn a little more. Whilst the athlete learns much from the coach, the good coach learns a little more from each athlete.

The good coach possesses a fair basis of knowledge and is constantly seeking more knowledge. He is reflective and is able to distinguish between fact and myth in athletics, between long based empiricism and 'gimmick'. He coaches from sound basic knowledge, but occasionally seeks to further practical coaching by judicious experiment. He also seeks information from the related fields of physiology, mechanics and psychology. However, in learning from these fields he must always consider the relevance of the information to his own coaching. He is not obsessed by pockets of knowledge but sees the value of selected information in its application to his coaching.

EXAMINATION FOR B.A.A.B. ASSISTANT CLUB COACH

Definition. A B.A.A.B. Assistant Club Coach is one who:
   (a) Will assist in the coaching of athletes.
   (b) Will not be considered qualified to assist in the coaching of athletes for fees.

Assessment. To be held periodically in each Area as and when required.

Assessors. A National Coach or selected B.A.A.B. Senior Coach.

Type. Practical assessment and discussion.

Procedure. The Assessment may be taken in any one or more of the following groups: Runs, Jumps, Throws, Hurdles, and Steeplechase.

Results. Results of Assessment will be notified to all candidates by the appropriate Joint Coaching Committee.

Fees. £1.00 per Assessment, to be submitted with application form.

Eligibility. Candidates must be at least 18 years of age.

Applications. Candidates should apply to the Honorary Secretary of the appropriate Joint Coaching Committee who will provide application form for completion and inform date, venue and time of Assessment.

Syllabus.
   1.   Knowledge of the basic elements of technique which will enable the Coach to work with novices in the rudiments of

a group of events.
2. Knowledge of the Rules and Safety procedures relating to a group of events and their application.
3. Knowledge of the 5 Star or Thistle Award Scheme.

Method of Assessment.
   (a) The candidate will be observed working in a Club situation assisting in the coaching of athletes;
   (b) Discussion will take place on the candidate's knowledge of the Syllabus;
   (c) Where large numbers of candidates are involved, the examiners may employ by agreement with the candidate a simple form of written or oral quiz.

Re-assessment. Failed candidates may apply for re-assessment at any time after six months from the date of their last attempt.

Badges. Candidates who are successful in qualifying as a B.A.A.B. Assistant Club Coach may wear the appropriate B.A.A.B. Badge obtainable from the B.A.A.B. Coaching Office.

0829799

3 Coaching – Practical Aspects

1. TECHNICAL EVENTS

Assuming that the coach possesses adequate technical knowledge of an event and of the ancillary aspects of training, he must then say to himself:

'How can I best help the athlete?'

Firstly the coach requires to know which main points about the event need to be passed on to the athlete *at the time*.

He may

(a) Demonstrate to the athlete, drawing attention to salient features. (But he must be aware of the fact that because he can perform competently it does not necessarily follow that he can *interpret* the event.)

(b) Persuade an expert to demonstrate, with the coach commenting on and drawing attention to salient features of the event.

(c) Verbally instruct. Occasionally it helps to have the athlete talk about and think about the technique of the event.

(d) Use diagrams and models.

(e) Use pictures of good athletes and slow motion films.

(f) Train with the athlete.

Useful coaching aids include the use of still photographs of the athlete – preferably sequence stills, which are the shots taken of one (say) jump at intervals of one-twentieth of a second.

Occasionally the coach may wish to tape record during a session, noting his own comments for later use. He may even tape comments from other coaches or top athletes for later instructional use with the athletes that he helps.

8 millimetre movie films of athletes can also be of value, and these are relatively inexpensive.

16 millimetre movie films can also be taken. Shown on a 'Specto' projector, the resultant films can be slowed down to 2 frames per second or stopped as 'still' shots. From the point of view of analysis this is extremely valuable, and points that have been made by the coach are brought vividly into perspective when the athlete sees his own performance. The disadvantage is that the 'Specto' projectors are relatively costly. It is also extremely valuable for the athlete to see loop shots of skilled performers and to compare their form with his own. But it is equally important that neither coach nor athlete become obsessed with niceties of technique. Events in athletics are 'wholes' and the coach should not over-emphasise the breakdown into parts which is only too apparent with the constant viewing of loop films.

Technique coaching on the track is as much an art as a science. If the coach understands the technique of an event, then in his practical coaching he needs to ask himself:

(a) What impression do I get from the performance as a whole? What is mechanically important, rather than what is stylishly interesting?
(b) Following this 'whole impression', what are the key features of the event?
(c) Where should I stand in order to see the important points?
(d) What major faults are likely to be seen? And what are the corrections for those faults?
(e) What should the athlete work on first? And how can I best explain to the athlete what the correct movements feel like? How do I interpret technique into meaningful aims for the athlete?

The coach should constantly strive to help the athlete to interpret his sensations. The athlete who stands at the end of a long jump runway with a blank mind may have many interesting moments in athletics – but he will experience few successes. The athlete who eventually succeeds in the acquisition of the skill of long jumping is the one who stands at the end of the runway in a training session and who works on one or two specific points of technique. He thinks before the jump, concentrating on the factor or factors which lead to success. He remembers the sensations of the successful jumps, and constantly strives to recapture those sensations. He remembers the sensations of the poor jumps, and constantly strives to eliminate those sensations. Often the coach will assist in the differentiation between good and bad. The coach also stresses the importance of purposeful repetition of one or two points – of the importance of the word '*Again*'.

It is also part of the coach's job to spot the technical faults, decide what to work on first and decide how to help the athlete overcome the faults. When a number of faults are evident it is usually best to work on one or two points to the exclusion of other points. To tell an athlete that he has many technical faults would be depressing for him. In general the coach's approach to a technical session should be to work to help the athlete improve one or two aspects of his performance, and to give adequate credit for the improvement of those aspects. Coaching should be positive, and praise is more effective than blame. During a training session some faults can be ignored whilst coach and athlete work to eliminate other faults. The athlete should finish the session feeling that he has worked on and shown improvement in certain worthwhile aspects of his performance. The coach should also remember that it is often as valuable to work to improve the athlete's strong points as it is to eliminate his weaknesses.

The Coaching Session

The coaching session should be a major event for both coach and athlete. Whilst the two may *coincide* at the track twice a week, it is improbable that the athlete will be coached on both occasions. The coach will *see* the athlete training but will not necessarily be involved in coaching him. On the actual coaching sessions, which may take place once a week or once a fortnight, the session will start with the athlete warmed-up and

FIG. 2.   THE WARM-UP

ready to commence training at a set time. The warm-up will commence with easy jogging suppling exercises, then striding and then some sharper bursts. If the athlete is concerned with a technical event then the final part of his warm-up will be related to the event – perhaps easy throws, or starts from blocks over 2 or 4 hurdles. Unless the weather is exceptionally warm,

B

he will wear his track suit throughout the warm-up, and will only take off his track suit at the suggestion of the coach. The coach will normally observe the final part of the warm-up, for from this he may learn something about the athlete's frame of mind and physical condition.

The good coaching session, like the good lesson, has an enjoyable beginning, a demanding middle section and a happy ending! The coach must come to the track with a prepared plan of training and a clear idea of the attitude of mind that he wishes to develop in the athlete. He will, however, be prepared to modify his plan in the light of special circumstances. His manner will be pleasant and purposeful. The athlete will be keen but apprehensive – keen to glean what information and inspiration he can, but apprehensive of the anticipated work load and of the coach's appraisal of his condition.

The coach's initial comments will be chosen to put the athlete at his ease. The coach will probably comment on progress to date and on plans for the immediate future. The main section of the training will be demanding in terms of either the physical effort required or in terms of the application and thought needed to acquire the complicated skills of the event. The coach's approach must be positive and encouraging, and there must be reinforcement of the athlete's striving for success. Only rarely will the coach criticise destructively. The session should finish on a good note, with the athlete feeling that his efforts have been wisely applied. The coach should keep a record of progress, and should give clear directions as to future work. This will often take the form of a typed schedule with one copy for the athlete and one for the coach.

2. COACHING – NON-TECHNICAL

Not all coaching is concerned with technique. In middle distance running, for instance, the coach may be more concerned with conditioning and tactics rather than with technique. Certainly the coach can advise in all events with regard to the acceptance and rejection of competition. He will also advise and possibly direct in the planning of the training schedule, aiming to balance out the apportionment of work on technique, stamina, speed and strength.

In rather more subtle ways the coach will need to indicate training needs to the athlete, for a change in training plans is more readily acceptable when the athlete feels the need for change. We must note here that many athletes train as they *like* to train and not always as they *need* to train. The coach can indicate these needs to the athlete by testing and by comparision with the performances of other athletes. Sometimes it suffices to have the athlete train in different company, for he will then clearly appreciate weaknesses.

The coach also needs to judge the athlete in training. Should the athlete now 'ease up and speed up'? Or does he need further conditioning work? Occasionally the coach needs to 'kid' the athlete – but only occasionally. The coach also needs to note that some technical weaknesses are solely the result of physical limitations, some of which can be ameliorated by appropriate conditioning work. The transmission of technical knowledge is of considerable importance, and it is vital that the coach can differentiate between the important and the unimportant, between technique and style. The coach must also talk a language that the athlete can understand. One of the most important qualities of the coach is the ability to interpret movements into sensations that have a concept for the athlete.

The Coach-Athlete Relationship

The role of the coach is firstly that he is available, that he will be there at the track, will welcome the athlete and will be fair and consistent. The good coach will be something of a lay-psychologist, keenly assessing the moods of the athlete, the needs of the occasion and the variations of approach suited to the athlete on that day. At all times he will be a friend, judge, listener and disciplinarian. Occasionally he may need to bully. It follows from the above that he will need some of the qualities of an actor!

Relationships involve responsibilities, and the responsibilities of the coach are firstly that he will coach and try to develop the athlete to the best of his ability. This will probably involve meeting with the athlete weekly or fortnightly for a coaching session. It has been argued that to see an athlete much less than this means that you are not really coaching but merely advising the athlete. We must note here that advice may be all that the experienced athlete needs after working with the coach over a number of years. For the coach to see the athlete too frequently may mean that the athlete will become too dependent upon the coach, and this is not good for the athlete. As has been noted previously, the aim of the coach is to help the athlete to become independent. If the coach takes all the decisions all of the time then the athlete may feel lost in the absence of the coach, and may be unable to cope. The coach should help the athlete along the road to taking his own decisions. So – even if you are at the track three times a week – only have your formal coaching sessions with a particular athlete on one of these occasions.

Even though the coach may only be holding a formal coaching session once a week, he must remember that in the coach-athlete relationship his main responsibility is to coach. This may mean hours of work in the rain and snow of Winter and Spring, for it is during this period that the foundations of summer successes are laid. When training becomes less important (because of imminent competition) the role of the coach becomes closer to that of an adviser. He should plan to influence the athlete into taking the right decisions, but yet to have the athlete feel that they are his own decisions.

It is during the late Winter and Spring build-up period that the athlete has the greatest need of the coach, for this is when the season seems so distant and the training so hard. When the summer comes the coach will fade into the background of the athlete's mind, and the coach must accept this. *The coach is working to help the athlete rather than the athlete working to help the coach.* The coach who constantly seeks the limelight, who is always there at the finish (fighting for television coverage) must search his mind for his motives in coaching. If it is for self-glory, then he is merely using the athletes as his stage.

Honesty and integrity are essential qualities of the coach, and his enthusiasms are those of the man wishing to develop athletes for their own sake. This will lead to mutual confidence and mutual respect, to a relationship that is essentially educational. The coach must respect the essential 'otherness' of the athlete, for no coach should try to pattern an athlete into a set mould. Initially the coach accepts the athlete as he is. From his starting point the coach tries to build upon the latent qualities of the athlete, eventually aiming to develop his maximum potential.

Relationships demand responsibilities from both coach and athlete. Perhaps the responsibilities of the coach are the greater, whilst the rewards are generally less. However, the athlete also has responsibilities, and unless he is prepared to accept these responsibilities he has no place on the coach's squad of athletes.

Firstly, the athlete must be reliable. He must be at the track, warmed up on time. If by any chance he cannot be there for an agreed session then he must notify the coach well in advance. If he misses a session without a very sound reason then he must be dropped from the squad. He may be the greatest physical material in the world, but if he lacks the qualities of reliability and perseverance then he is not worth coaching. Of course we hope that he stays in athletics and enjoys the sport ... but he just is not worthy of the coach's time. Time could be money: if you choose to coach, then, by the same token, you choose to give up earnings or recreation. To coach is only worthwhile if the athletes are reliable. This rule is inflexible. If you are prepared to devote time and effort to the athlete then he must be reliable. Neither must the coach mollycoddle the athletes. The beginning of any coaching relationship is that the athlete must be prepared to meet the demands of the coach, the first of which is that the athlete must always be there and on time.

Secondly, the athlete must do as he is told. Initially this seems to be a harsh dictum, but it is a necessary one for the young athlete to accept. Initially the coach dictates, whilst at a later stage he will discuss and advise.

Thirdly, the athlete must be coachable. He must follow instructions during the training session and must follow a directed plan of training between visits from the coach. The coach will set work from one visit until the next, and the athlete must work through this schedule and keep a precise record of that work.

It is *hoped* that the athlete will show his appreciation for the help that he has received. Athletes are almost always appreciative of coaching help and usually acknowledge this help. The coach, however, must not *expect* private or public thanks. The mature coach can accept this for he is aware of the selfish streak possessed by most athletes. The coach also knows that towards the end of formal coach-athlete relationship, he has developed the athlete to a maturity in which there is little need for the coach.

Whilst we all enjoy acclaim for our efforts, we must accept that not all coaches will receive the acclaim due to them. The wise coach will accept this with equanimity.

Taking on the athlete

Every coach experiences the situation in which he meets a youngster of undoubted physical potential and immediately feels that he can help this youngster along the road to athletic success.

The first step in taking on an athlete is to ensure that no one else is coaching him! Too often in athletics we find that there are problems of who is coaching whom, and the coach must be wary of offering assistance to an athlete who already has a coach. Assuming that the athlete in question is not being coached and obviously wants coaching assistance then the coach must consider the situation objectively. He must ask himself if he

1. Has enough knowledge of the event.
2. Has the time to coach the athlete.
3. Has access to suitable facilities.

With some athletes the coach must even suggest that another coach has more to offer them in terms of event-knowledge.

If the answers to the above questions are favourable, then the coach must think of the coach-athlete relationship. Coaching, like marriage, demands compatibility. One of the problems here is that until the coach has worked with the athlete for some weeks it will not be possible to find out how well they 'get on'. Probably the best solution is to be non-committal in the first instance and simply to invite the athlete along to a training session to work out with other athletes. In this situation you (the coach) can see how the athlete reacts to training, to advice and to hard work. You can also attempt to assess him as a person. You can talk with him about his training problems and gauge the extent to which he is prepared to plan for the future. You can also assess the extent to which he fits in with the rest of your squad. If you are satisfied on these counts then you can offer to coach him, stating your requirements. If the athlete is prepared to abide by these requirements then you might agree to coach for, perhaps, a 6 months trial period. At the end of this you can then decide whether or not to continue – and the decision is as much that of the athlete as of the coach. If you wish to continue the coaching relationship from this point, then the athlete should be given a fair indication of his potential and expected rate of progress, and of how much time he is expected to devote to the sport.

Where do you find the athletes? In the main the athletes that you take on are youngsters who are already involved in the sport. Occasionally, however, you might tempt a youngster from another sport. Very often a soccer player might make, say, a first class long jumper. A gymnast might make a good pole vaulter. Basically, however, you do not find athletes, they find you. Though few athletes are likely to say, 'Will you coach me?' (for they would fear rejection), there are many who will, by conversation with you or by association with the athletes that you already help, indicate a desire to join your squad.

You must not allow your squad to become too large. Normally the coach can expect to work effectively with a maximum of 8–10 athletes. Effective coaching makes demands of time and emotion upon the coach, and the coach (like the athlete) must limit athletics to being a reasonable part of his life. Coaching is much more than techniques and schedules, for it involves a consideration of the wide range of problems of the athlete. To coach effectively the coach must know his athletes extremely well. He must study them and must try to understand them as individuals, as people, and not merely as athletes.

Because of the intimacy of the coach-athlete relationship, the responsibilities of the coach are considerable. His educational influence is great, for he affects the attitudes of the athlete to things other than athletics. The coach must help the athlete to keep the sport in perspective and also help to keep the athlete's eyes focused upon home and career commitments. The coach may commence the coach-athlete relationship as an athletics mentor, a father-figure and possibly careers master. He should finish the coaching relationship as a respected friend.

The aim of the coach is to guide the young athlete to an athletics career in which the athlete eventually achieves the best performance of which he is capable. The coach also aims to produce an athlete who has improved professionally, who is independent of the coach and who is a gentleman. To coach is also to educate.

1. Resistance running – international canoeist K. Langford

2. Resistance running – English Schools Steeplechase Champion S. Hollings

3. Leg Press

4. Dips (parallel bars) and Weighted Chins

4 Fitness for Athletics

The athlete must see his sport in perspective. He must place his career before his athletics, but should then be prepared to devote a minimum of four hours a week to intensive training. Because there are limitations of time to be spent on training, this time must be used to the best advantage. In short, it must be planned. The athlete must aim to push his performance to the limit of his ability, and to harness his physical and intellectual abilities over a number of years, in order to achieve excellence.

The problem of the coach is to advise the athlete *how best to use limited time in order to maximise his potential and achieve excellence.*

How to do this? On the basis of animal fitness – to be maintained throughout the year – the athlete is trying to build specific 'fitnesses'. The anticipated result will be physical excellence and resultant confidence.

The athlete will aim to develop qualities of:

Strength
Skill
Stamina
Speed
Suppleness

and excellence in these qualities will lead to good mental condition. The coach will base his selection from the above qualities upon

(a) The time of the year.
(b) The event

(c) The individual athlete.

Before thinking of specific training plans, however, there are a number of factors to be considered.

Food

1. Meals should be taken regularly. The final meal before a competition or very hard training session should be taken at least three hours previous to competition or training.

2. Carbohydrate (sugars: starch) intake should be increased before racing. A middle distance or long distance runner should stop heavy training at least 48 hours before competition in order to allow the body's store of carbohydrates to build up.

3. First class proteins (meat, fish, eggs, cheese, milk) must be taken by the athlete, for proteins contain the amino acids necessary for life and growth. Excessive protein intake will not increase performance, however.

4. The intake of vitamins must be regular and must be over and above a required minimum, for the body cannot store every type of vitamin. Vitamin C deficiency, for instance, weakens the resistance of the body to colds and minor infections, and Vitamin B deficiency results in fatigue. In the case of Vitamin B there is some argument for supplementing the diet in order to decrease the liability to fatigue of the central nervous system.

Vitamin A is found in carrots, egg yolk, apricots, tomatoes.

Vitamin B_1 is found in yeast and yeast extracts, in dried peas, beans, lentils, green vegetables etc.

Vitamin B_2 is found in cheese, fish roe, kidney, liver, green vegetables etc.

Vitamin C is found in citrus fruits, raw vegetables etc.

The coach should check to see that the athlete's diet is reasonably well balanced. In rare cases he may need to make certain recommendations, but in almost all cases he will find that the present high standard of living means that athletes eat well. If the coach should suspect any dietary problems he should first check a sensible book on diet (there are many). He might also wish to check with an expert (say, a teacher of Home

Economics). Physical ailments or excessive liability to fatigue should be referred to a doctor.

Sleep

The athlete must have adequate sleep at all times. 'Adequate', however, varies considerably from athlete to athlete, and the athlete's own criterion will be his own sense of well-being. If the coach finds that the athlete is tiring rapidly in a training session he is advised to check on sleep.

When travelling with teams and when at home the athlete needs a well ventilated room, preferably free from noise. It is noise that keeps athletes awake, and when travelling the athlete should try to avoid the hotel rooms overlooking busy streets. The old adage 'An hour in before midnight is worth two afterwards' is a good one. Occasionally, however, the coach may need to advise an athlete to stay up a little later on the night before a competition in order to ensure that he becomes tired enough to sleep well. In this situation an additional hour's lie in would be recommended for the following morning.

Basic Fitness, to the layman, might simply be considered to be the absence of illness and the ability to perform one's work. Certainly absence of illness is essential to the athlete. In the event of problems of physical condition a check should be made with the athletes General Practitioner. The athlete should take dental checks at intervals of six months.

To the athlete, basic fitness means much more than the absence of ill-health. Fitness to the athlete is positive and represents the ability to sustain work without undue stress. The constituents of this basic fitness are running and strength training, and, in some form, these two factors should be developed by all athletes. Throwers may feel that there is little need to run – but they should remember that they are athletes before they are throwers, and that great throwers are rarely limited to one event. Long distance runners may not feel the need for strength work, but the same argument of general fitness preceding specific work holds good. There appear to be no disadvantages in a long distance runner being reasonably strong, and there probably are advantages.

*   *   *

RUNNING TRAINING FOR GENERAL FITNESS USUALLY
TAKES ONE OF FOUR FORMS

1. *Steady running.* An unfit novice might be advised to start
his training by simply running for five minutes. Eventually he
should build up to the stage at which he is capable of running
slowly for 15 minutes. This probably represents a low base of
running fitness upon which he can build more intensive forms
of training.

2. *Fartlek* (from the Swedish 'speed-play') which involves
varied running – fast strides, jogging, sprint bursts, preferably
over soft undulating country. The athlete runs as the spirit takes
him and as the countryside demands. Fartlek runs are gauged
in terms of time without reference to distance. An athlete's
schedule might include 30 minutes fartlek.

3. *Interval work,* which consists of alternating periods of
work load and recovery in which we can approximately define
the intensity of the stimulus, the duration of the effort and the
recovery period between efforts.

Interval work is mainly the preserve of runners and hurdlers,
and will be dealt with in some detail under the heading 'Middle-
distance running'. Nevertheless jumpers are advised to do some
interval training during the spring and early summer period.
Throwers will also benefit from this work.

4. *Resistance running* forms the basis for some of the athlete's
winter training. The general principle is to make the running
more difficult. The athlete accepts that the form of the running
may be rather different from his event, but he uses resistance
running in an attempt to improve his stamina, or his strength
or possibly both of these factors.

Forms of resistance running:
  Sandhill running.
  Repetition uphill sprints.
  Cross country running and racing.
  Running through snow.
  Running wearing a weighted belt.
  Sprints against resistance (A harness held by other athletes,
  or a harness fixed to a heavy motor tyre.)
  Sprints pulling a garden roller.

In general, resistance running would be utilised perhaps once a week, and the form might be varied. Some aspects of resistance running (e.g. sandhill work) can form the focal point for a useful week-end squad gathering.

STRENGTH TRAINING for general fitness and strength training for the specific demands of certain events can be developed by means of:

Progressive Resistance Exercises
It is possible to plan some useful strength training simply using the weight of the body and by performing such exercises as:
  Sit-ups.
  Press-ups, and press-ups from a handstand position. (i.e. handstand against a wall)
  Rope climb
  Pull-ups on a beam (also known as 'Chins')
  Dips between parallel bars.
  Single leg squats.
With exercises of the type, progress can be maintained in various ways:
  By lengthening the lever.
  By increasing the speed of movement.
  By altering the starting position
  By increasing the number of repetitions.
The coach will think of ways of increasing the work load, often by having the exercise performed more times or from a more difficult position.

WEIGHT TRAINING, however, is the commonest way of developing strength. Research has shown that weight training is an effective method of improving strength. The majority of athletes find weight training to be satisfying, for they can see progress.
The weight trainer uses a certain number of
  Repetitions – the number of times that an exercise is performed without an intervening break.
  Sets – the number of groups of repetitions.

FIG. 3.   SINGLE LEG SQUAT

FIG. 4.   SINGLE ARM BICEP CHIN

Part of a weight trainer's schedule, for instance, might be listed as:

Press   100 lb   8 x 3 (i.e. 8 repetitions, 3 sets)

The 3 set system of 8 repetitions is the safe system to introduce to youngsters and this is recommended for the first 8–10 weeks of weight training.

Ultimately, however, strength is best improved by the use of *heavy weights* and a *low number of repetitions.* The athlete noted above would probably move on to:

Press   120 lb   4 x 4

At an even later stage he would probably move on to the 'Pyramid' system of training, e.g.

Press   120 lbs   4 x 2
             125 lb   3 x 2
             130 lb   2 x 2
             135 lb attempt. (with 'spotters' available)

Organising the Weight training schedule
The requirements of the athlete are:
1. All-round strength – and this necessitates work for
       Legs
       Upper body
       Abdominals
2. The athlete may sometimes need specific strengths, and may need to include in his schedule exercises specific to the event. Thus the pole vaulter might include in his schedule:
    Pull-ups 40 lb tied to feet   6 x 3
3. The ability to *attack* the weights as the athlete would attack his event. In addition to regular repetition movements there is a place for over-all dynamic movements, such as the 'Snatch' or the Power Clean.

The coach must bear in mind the importance of:
1. Purpose and plan in strength training. The athlete should keep a training diary for all his training and not merely his event.
2. The correct performance of exercises.
3. *Safety* (a) Weights firmly fixed to the bar.
              (b) 'Spotters' to be available when the athlete is attempting maximum lifts.
4. *Not* working against time. Exercises done against time may have more cardio-vascular than strength demands. But this does not mean that the weight training session should drag on for two hours or so!

5. Working to a maximum, but not working the same muscle groups on consecutive days.
6. Occasional variation and competition to maintain interest.

How often?
As a general guide
3 times a week in winter and early spring.
Twice a week in late spring and early summer.
Once a week during peak season, the weight training sessions to be well clear of competition. During the peak season period the athlete will maintain poundages but will reduce both sets and repetitions. His aim will be simply to 'stay in touch' with the weights.
It must be noted, however, that the student may need to limit his weight training sessions to twice a week even during the winter. Demands of time vary from individual to individual.

Middle distance runners would be ill-advised to *substitute* weight training for running. They should do some weight training in addition to running. Middle-distance runners often use 'split session' training, doing some work with weights before going out on a training run and the remainder of the weight session upon returning from the run.

Bearing in mind the above principles, here is a suggested weight training schedule for a 17 year old hurdler. It is assumed that he has one year of weight training experience and that his body weight is 160 lb.

Warm up:
    1. Full range of suppling and stretching exercises.
    2. Clean and Press   70 lb   10 x 2
Then:
    1. Bicep curl (cheat)   90 lb   6 x 3
    2. Behind neck Press   90 lb   6 x 3
    3. Sit-ups on   10 lb   8 x 2
       inclined bench   behind
                          neck.

FIG. 5. BICEP CURL

FIG. 6. SIT-UP – INCLINED BENCH

FIG. 7. BENCH PRESS

FIG. 8. STEP UPS

FIG. 9. POWER CLEAN
*Note the flat back and the straight
arms. Eyes looking forwards*

4. Bench Press	100 lb	6 x 2
	110 lb	4 x 2
	120 lb	2 x 2
	125 lb	1 attempt.
5. Step-ups on to 16″ bench.	125 lb	10 x 3 (5 left foot lead 5 right)
6. Snatch *or* Power Clean		6 attempts.

(Note that in a 'cheat' bicep curl the athlete does not limit the movement to the work of the biceps. He swings the body back as he curls the weight.)

Weight lifting – a sport in its own right – is an important adjunct to weight training. The three Olympic lifts are:

    Clean and Press
    Snatch
    Clean and Jerk.

Some athletes train primarily on the Olympic lifts and many 'heavy event' athletes are competent competitive weight lifters.

Actual work out of a 200' hammer thrower. Warm up then:

Press	Snatch	Clean and Jerk	Squat
155 x 3	155 x 3	225 x 3	265 x 5
175 x 3	175 x 3	235 x 3	305 x 5
185 x 3	185 x 3	245 x 3	325 x 5
195 x 3	195 x 3	255 x 2	340 x 5
205 x 3	205 x 1	265 x 2	
215 x 2	205 x 1		
225 x 1		Weights in pounds.	

Performance on the Olympic lifts form a useful guide to the strength of the athletes. It must be noted, however, that they are not lifts of pure strength because a considerable skill element is involved. Coaches often organise weight lifting competitions for their athletes during the out-of-season period, for the coach appreciates that most athletes thrive both emotionally and socially on competition. For the reasonably skilled lifters the Olympic lifts are ideal. For other weight trainers, competitions can be organised using, for instance, the simpler lifts of Power Clean or Bench Press.

As a rough guide the coach might set targets for his athletes in the power events on the basis of:

Press	Body weight
Snatch	Body weight
Clean and Jerk	Body weight x 1.33
Bench Press	Body weight x 1.33
Power Clean	Body weight x 1.33

The targets will obviously vary from individual to individual.

ISOMETRIC TRAINING involves tension but negligible movement. Isometrics can be thought of as being 'static contractions'. Isometrics have been used instead of weight training.

Advantages of Isometrics
   (a) Economical of time
   (b) No special equipment is needed – improvisation is simple.

Disadvantages of Isometrics

    (a) Not as satisfying as weight training.

    (b) Strength developed in movement seems to be preferable to that developed in isometrics. A pole vaulter, for instance, might best develop strength through a combination of weight training, body resistance work (e.g. rope climb, chins) and strength developed in the swinging movements of Olympic gymnastics.

The athlete's best plan is to take out an 'insurance policy' and add some isometric work to his weight training.

Isometric contractions are held maximally and briefly, usually for a period of approximately six seconds. They are made in a range of positions, some against the resistance of self and other against an immovable object.

Examples:

Isometrics against an object

    'Press' against the top of a door frame.

    Push against the side of a door frame.

    Sit on a chair and attempt to lift the seat up.

    Attempt a single arm chin.

Isometrics against self

    Attempt a bicep curl against the resistance of the other hand.

    Push against the other hand.

    Pull against the other hand.

CIRCUIT TRAINING involves the completion of a certain number of exercises within a limited time. The improved physical condition resultant from circuit training really comes under the heading of 'being in good shape'. Circuit training is a form of training perhaps more suited to games players than to athletes. However, at the level of club athletics, circuit training is an excellent 'conditioner' and a means of gathering a group together for enjoyable hard work.

In circuit training the apparatus used is spaced round the gymnasium and there is usually a card illustrating each exercise and indicating the number of times that the exercise must be done. Often there are circuits of different severity, e.g.

FIG. 10.   ISOMETRICS

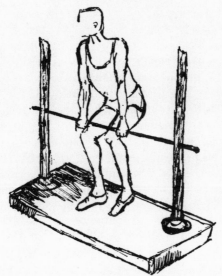

FIG. 11.   ISOMETRICS

'Easy' circuit	6 sit-ups	Green circuit
'Medium' circuit	8 sit-ups	Blue circuit
'Difficult' circuit	10 sit-ups	Red circuit.

An example of a circuit might be:

	Circuit		
	Green	*Blue*	*Red*
1. Jump Chins	4	6	8
2. Step-ups	12	15	20
			(Step-ups on to 2 benches)
3. Trunk curls	8	10	12
4. Clean and Press	8 @ 60 lb	6 @ 80 lb	8 @ 80 lb
5. Dorsal raise with medicine ball behind neck	6	8	10
6. Press-ups	6	8	10 with thumbs touching
7. Shuttle sprints	3	5	6

In circuit training the athlete works his way round the gym once: then again: then a 3rd time. As soon as he is able to complete the 'Easy' circuit in less than a set time he will progress (for his next training session) to the medium circuit.

A second form of circuit training is based on the individual. The athlete comes to the gymnasium for the first autumn session and is tested to maximum on each activity. 'Maximum' refers to the greatest number of say, chins to exhaustion *or* to the greatest number of efforts that he can manage in one minute. In both cases his work dose will be 50 per cent of the achieved score, and the athlete notes this down on his circuit card. This is his circuit, and he works to this circuit for perhaps six weeks. Then he is tested again and starts again on a fresh work load.

A third form of circuit is essentially coach directed throughout. This is the 'time circuit'. The coach dictates that all athletes work for (say) 20 seconds on an activity. Then there is a brief rest period before the athlete starts work on the next activity, again working maximally . . . and so on.

5 Planning the Training Schedule

Following a brief lay-off at the end of the season, the schedule of training would probably start in October, build up gradually during the winter and spring before tapering off for the peak season competitions. A coach would normally start working with a new athlete in October, planning for the following season. It is usually unwise to start to coach an athlete in the mid-season period, for to do so might do more harm than good.

The general plan of training – applicable to all events – is shown in Fig. 12, width of the lines showing quatity of work.

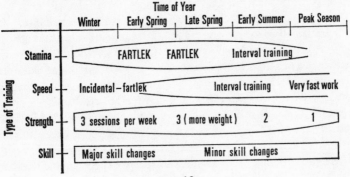

FIG. 12

The general plan for background physical work – be it stamina work for the runners or strength work for the throwers – is to build up during the out-of-season period and simply maintain during the season. As stamina or strength work is reduced, so speed work is increased. The period of greatest overlap occurs during the late spring which is the immediate pre-season period. This is when the athlete is producing the

55

greatest quantity of work. Eventually, however, quantity gives way to the quality work of summer. The athlete then feels that training is less demanding, and he approaches competitions with eagerness.

Of the four factors considered above, the skill element is seen to be constant throughout. Yet, whilst the athlete may be working on the skill of an event for perhaps 11 months of the year, the *emphasis* varies. During the out-of-season period the athlete may be working on major skill changes, whilst during the early season he will only be making minor modifications to his technique. During the peak season it is unlikely that the athlete will make any changes, for his skill work will represent consolidation.

Skill training requires considerable mental effort from the athlete. He needs to be aware of what he is trying to achieve and constantly to reflect on the feeling of movements. He should know the rules of the event and the key features of the event. He should appreciate the technical requirements of the event, but should not be obsessed with minor points. The coach will focus the attention of the athlete upon selected aspects of skill performance during the training session. He will help the athlete to interpret the sensations of that performance, by observing, questioning and directing the athlete's 'mental set'.

The athlete will have to follow up some aspects of skill work when the coach is not present. This is good for the athlete, for he *must* be able, in a sense, to coach himself. Such a training session would include work in which the athlete had been given specific aims. When no coach is available to watch him, the athlete might occasionally persuade someone to act as a mirror for him. He would ask them to watch specific and easily observable points. The athlete can rarely expect another athlete to be an expert, but he can expect the astute observer to watch and comment upon specific, clearly explained points. Just to have someone watch, say, two or three jumps at the beginning of a session can often give the athlete a clear line of attack for the remainder of the session. If an athlete is fortunate enough to train with another athlete who is a competent and intelligent performer in the same event then much mutual coaching should occur.

5. 'Spotters' standing by for the Two-handed Snatch

6. Isometrics

7, 8, 9. Circuit training at Madeley College

During training sessions on technique work one of the aims of the coach is to help the athlete to eliminate variables. Skill training should bring the athlete closer and closer to what is considered to be the ideal technique for that athlete.

For the athlete, the keynote is *efficiency*. Each training session is to be economical and planned. The coach would normally plan for schedules to be changed each fortnight, thus helping to maintain both interest and progress.

Efficiency means that time spent in training is important and not just time spent at the track. Whilst it is hoped that the athlete will be sociable, this sociability should not interfere with the main purpose of the visit to the track, which is to *train*.

The athlete should keep a training diary (see page 56). This should be a record of both training and competition, which must be made available for the coach to inspect. The training diary is a useful guide to the suitability of various training modifications, and provides an incentive to the athlete . . . it's bad to see the blank pages! The athlete needs to maintain a rhythm of training throughout the year with but a brief break from athletics. During this break from the sport he should continue with some form of exercise, probably recreative activitives as part of the end-of-season holiday.

Training schedules are designed to suit the individual. What may suit one athlete could cause something close to a physical breakdown with another athlete. The coach plans schedules for an athlete on the basis of what he knows about the athlete and about the event. The coach who posts schedules to an athlete that he does not know is not coaching but merely advising. Furthermore his advice is based only on the event and not on the athlete. You cannot coach by post.

Training Schedules – General Principles

1. The schedule is built upon knowledge of

    (a) the event
    (b) the athlete's physical and mental make up
    (c) previous training and conditioning.

2. The build up should be gradual.

3. The athlete should not be working to maximum in similar

TRAINING

March 1967 Day and Date	Woke at	STRENGTH	RUNNING	SKILL	Comments or other activity	Bed at
Sun. 19th	8.30		30 minutes Fartlek		2 hours digging!	11.00
Mon. 20th	7.30	Press 120 4 × 3 Curl 100 6 × 3 Abd. 10 × 2 Clean 150 4 × 4 Step-ups 200 12 × 2		20 'pop-ups' from 40' approach: 80m low hurdles × 6	Fair height from board but not keeping body upright	10.30
Tues. 21st	7.30				Basketball match	10.45
Wed. 22nd	7.45		150m strides × 6	Repetition hopping until tired		11.00
Thurs. 23rd	7.30	Snatch 130 lb. Press 125 lb. Clean and Jerk 165 lb.	20 minutes easy run		Weight lifting trial – best total to date!	10.45
Fri. 24th	7.30					10.45
Sat. 25th		Weight Training as on Monday	80m v. fast strides × 4	20' 6" jump from 11 stride approach	Take-off not well timed: only 1 good jump Cut Wt. sessions to twice weekly	12.00

activities on consecutive days, for this might result in a breaking down rather than a building up.

4. The schedule must be planned to suit the time availability of the individual.

   There is in vogue a tendency for schedules to become increasingly severe, and this is not always justified. Because some training is good, it does not necessarily follow that more training is better. A considerable amount of work can be done in a short space of time, and the task of the coach is to balance judiciously the various facets of training into a whole which suits the individual and the training time available to that individual. Certainly there are athletes who have trained for less than 5 hours a week and have gained international vests in the mid 1960's.

5. The various aspects of training can often be done in one and the same training session. Thus a hurdler might work out on the track and then go immediately to a weight training session.

6. The essence of training is hard, purposeful work in a relatively short space of time.

A specimen schedule for a 17-year-old schoolboy jumper for late Spring might be:

Day	Schedule	Time (including minimum time for changing and showering)
Sunday	30 minutes fartlek	$\frac{3}{4}$
Monday	Technique work:	
	Weight training	$1\frac{1}{4}$
Tuesday	150m x 6 with 4 minute recovery	$\frac{3}{4}$
Wednesday	Weight training	$\frac{3}{4}$
Thursday	'Pop ups':	
	repetition very fast strides	$\frac{3}{4}$
Friday		
Saturday	Technique work (main session)	
	Supplementary strength training	$1\frac{1}{4}$

Hours per week $5\frac{1}{2}$

For the above schedule it is assumed that the boy concerned is working towards 'A' level examinations and that he is not involved in major games. For a boy who is required to play a major game once a week it would be acceptable to reduce the amount of running in the training schedule.

It is suggested that the athlete should continue to train throughout the period of build up to examinations and even through the examination period itself, for one cannot study all the time. During the period of intense mental effort, however, the athlete's approach to training will be rather different from his approach during, say, winter. Intensity of training at times demands a mental discipline which the athlete cannot spare during times of academic stress. During this latter critical period the athlete should treat athletics simply as a pleasurable pastime and not as a discipline. His aim should be to relax through athletics, bearing in mind that by 'staying in touch' he will quickly return to form after the examination period.

Training should be a pleasure, although it is at times the pleasure of disciplined hard work. The coach should plan for the schedule to be both demanding and interesting.

6 The Sprints

Sprinting is defined as

'Running at or close to maximum speed.'

Whilst an athlete may be able to hold his top speed but briefly, the very fit athlete is able to hold close to top speed for some distance. Thus the 100 metres is known as a pure sprint, and there is very little falling off from top speed. The 200 metres is close to being a pure sprint, but the athlete does not aim for maximum speed. The 400 metres, although run at slower speed controlling some of his running at marginally less than maximum speed. The 440 yards, although run a slower speed than either of the other two sprints, nevertheless comes into the category of a sprint: it is a sustained sprint.

Sprinting involves two major factors:

(a) How fast the sprinter can move his legs, and
(b) How long his stride is – normally 20–40% more than the athlete's standing height.

Sprinting is a combination of these two factors. In practice no way has yet been found of greatly influencing the first of these factors. Technique coaching in the sprints is directed towards maintaining cadence and, at the same time, increasing stride length.

Qualities of the Sprinter

Sprinters come in a variety of shapes and sizes: there are short, chunky sprinters, usually very fast over 40 metres but who have the problem of maintaining speed even in a short sprint. There are 'rangy' sprinters who may not be quite so sharp over, say, 20 metres but who continue to 'flow' during the latter stages of the race; and there are the bulky, powerful sprinters of the Hayes build. Yet they all give the impression of being 'sharp' in their running – they all have good leg speed.

Events vary in the extent to which the coach can help the athlete to improve. In general, the more technical events and the distance runs lend themselves to greater improvement through perseverance and coaching. In sprinting the limitations of natural ability are probably greater than in other events. In effect the club coach might be delighted with a 3 per cent improvement in a season from a club sprinter, whereas he would expect a far greater improvement from a hammer thrower at club level.

Key features

Assuming that the athlete possesses good leg speed, the key features of good sprinting are, in this order:

(a) Powerful leg drive, with extension of rear leg, balanced with

(b) An equally powerful arm drive, forward and back, with an angle of approximately 90 degrees as the arm is

FIG. 13.   THE SPRINT ACTION:
Leg drive, knee lift, arm drive

forward (there is some opening out of the elbow on the back swing of the arms).
(c) Good knee lift – a wide split between the thighs.
(d) No undue tension at speed.

The order of priority is significant. Firstly, the athlete must drive with the legs, and the coach will check for complete extension of the rear leg. This must be balanced out with an equally powerful arm drive. We must note that point (c) – knee lift – is of little value without the leg drive (taken to its ultimate this fault would be 'running on the spot' with high knee lift). The coach must check for leg drive and then for the wide split between the thighs which indicates knee lift *and* drive. Point (d) – relaxation – can only be of value as the culmination of other features of technique and fitness. To relax and run slowly is of no value to the sprinter, but to appear comfortable at speed is of considerable value.

Coaching
Coaching position (1) is from the side, perhaps 20 metres from the runner.

Major fault 1:
Inadequate leg drive – failure to extend rear leg.

Corrections:
(a) (Out-of-season)
Repetition uphill sprints, concentrating on leg drive.
(b) (In-season)
Rolling starts over 30 metres, increasing to 60 metres with the athlete thinking of 'Drive, drive'... thinking initially of the legs, then of the arms. (A 'rolling' start is one in which the athlete jogs to the start line and then drives away powerfully).
(c) Drive powerfully away and then try to *lead* with the arms rather than simply following the legs.

Major fault 2:
Lack of knee lift – an inefficient split of the legs resulting in lack of stride length.

Corrections:

(a) Check hip mobility – possibly prescribe mobility exercises, e.g.

   1. lunge position

   2. free swing of one leg

   3. hurdle rear leg action.

(b) Drive away from the start and then think of *maintaining* leg drive and adding knee lift.

Major fault 3:

Undue tension – noticeably in the neck.

   Correction:

(a) Plan for an adequate background of winter running.

(b) Hit full running speed and then try to relax and maintain speed: hit full speed then coach 'Smile'.

Coaching position (2) – not often used – is from the front or rear.

Major fault 4:

Rolling of shoulders from side to side.

   Correction:

Emphasise arm drive forwards and back.

Major fault 5:

Feet splayed or off line.

   Correction:

Concentrate on knee drive being 'in line' with the line of run. Note than 'off line' movements are wasteful movements. The coach might expect a little rolling in the first few strides away from the blocks, but thereafter the sprinter's feet should be pointing in line with the line of the run and should leave spike marks *just* at either side of a 2 inch line.

---

10.   4 x 100 m relay. Sharon Colyear hands over the baton to Anita Neil. The exchange has been a good one with adequate 'free distance' between the runners. Although the baton is out of alignment it has already left Colyear's hand. Note that Neil has grasped the baton in such a way that she has plenty of stick to hand to the next girl. (*Tony Duffy*)

(Photo: Tony Duffy)

(*Photo: Mark Shearman*)

11. European Championships 110 metres Hurdles, Budapest, 1966. This photograph of Heat 1, is complementary to Fig. 15C (*page 72*) showing the drive away from the hurdle. Both Ottoz (Italy) in the lead, followed by Hemery (Gt Britain), show excellent form in this respect

The Sprint Start

The requirements of a sprint start position are that

(a) It should be a position of balance.
(b) It should be a position from which the athlete can drive powerfully and at speed.
(c) It should be a position from which the athlete can achieve maximum speed as quickly as possible.

FIG. 14.   THE SPRINT START

We must note at this stage that the important factor in sprint starting is effective work at and from the blocks. If a sprinter has left the blocks before his opponents but has not driven powerfully from them, then he may be leading after one metre but may be well behind at 15 metres. This rates as a poor start. The athlete must drive away powerfully, in balance and smoothly into his sprinting. In coaching the start we need to do some of our coaching with the athlete running distances up to 80 metres. Certainly the athlete should do many starts in which he runs 50 metres, for the effectiveness of the start is not seen merely in the first 10 metres or so.

The Sprint position – Key features
  Hips slightly higher than shoulders
  Shoulders forward of the line
  A 'flattish' back
  Eyes looking about 60 cm. down the track
  Angles at knees – 90 degrees
  Angles at knees 115 degrees
  Angles of blocks – 45 degrees (front)
  Angles of blocks – 80 degrees (rear)

Coaching position (1), Side, 10 metres from athlete.

C

Arms straight   ⎫ Coaching
Hands shoulder width apart   ⎬ position (2),
Weight on high bridge of forefinger and thumb   ⎭ Front.

                ⎫ Coaching
Heels vertical ⎬ position (3),
                ⎭ Rear.

For the start on a bend (200 metres), the sprinter starts from the outside of his lane in order that he can run straight for the first (accelerating) part of the race.

With young athletes it is best to get them into a starting position that is approximately correct – this can be done quite quickly – and then to work on starts over some 40 metres. The athlete will then have the feeling of starting and moving at speed from blocks. In the beginning it is more important for the athlete is get a reasonable start, and to know what this feels like, than it is for him to spend too much time in aiming for the *perfect* starting position. Eventually, of course, the athlete will aim for perfection at all stages: then the coach will work through the points noted, checking from positions (1), (2) and (3). The coach must bear in mind that the recommended starting position is a guide, being the position generally considered to be the best. The coach may decide upon slight variations to suit the particular athlete.

The main fault that is likely to be seen in the starting position is that the athlete, having been allocated correct positions for the feet (40 cm. line to toe, 40 cm. between the front and rear foot) does not lean far enough forwards. This is probably due to physical weaknesses in the fingers and in the shoulder girdle. The correction here may need to be a long-term correction – to strengthen the upper body and fingers sufficiently so that the athlete can lean further forwards and take more weight on the fingers.

Faults in the starting position are relatively easy to correct, for the athlete should be stationary. Once these faults have been corrected, we then have to face the much more difficult task of correcting faults in the start itself. We must think of the start as being that period of the race during which the athlete is accelerating rapidly. In particular, the first 30 metres of the race.

The main coaching position is position (1A) which is opposite a point about 15 metres down the track and some 20 metres from the track itself. Some of the faults that the coach may note have already been listed under the heading of 'Sprinting': other faults likely to occur are:

Major fault 1:
Standing up and then running, instead of a gradual rise over a distance of approximately 15 metres.
   Correction:
   Drive powerfully (arms and legs) from the blocks *and* during the strides away from the blocks. Avoid lifting the head and eyes too quickly – initially look down the track and not at the finishing tape. Athlete to feel that he is driving the hips forward.

Major fault 2:
Stumbling out of blocks.
   Correction:
   (a) Check the block spacing.
   (b) Check that the head is not too far down in the start – some athletes make the mistake of looking back at the feet.
   (c) More practice. Smoothness should come as intelligent practice helps the athlete to acquire the skill.

Major fault 3:
'Pattering' away from the blocks.
   Correction:
   Athlete to think of 'Drive, drive' and of using the arms powerfully.

Major fault 4:
Slow 'reaction' to the gun.
   Correction:
   (a) Check the starting position.
   (b) Athlete to think of 'Running' and 'Driving', rather than of listening for the gun.

Major fault 5:
Early dip plus loss of form at finish.

Correction:
Run through tape!

Tactical considerations in the 400 metres

The aim of the athlete is to run the best race of which he is capable. There are no tactical problems of jockeying for position, of being 'barged' or of being 'boxed in'. The problems of the 400 metre runner, in the main, are problems of judging his own ability, having confidence in that judgement and the determination to justify that judgement. He needs to be able to assess the quality of performance that he is likely to return under the conditions prevailing on a particular day and then to judge his pace in order to get the best possible performance out of himself. He should not be unduly concerned with watching other runners, for he must be primarily concerned with his own race.

The athlete's main focus of attention will be upon a 'sharp' start and a very fast run round the first bend. He should then ease into a fast, comfortable stride down the back straight and gradually to build up effort round the final bend. As he comes off the final bend he will be driving at close to maximum effort, driving determinedly and striving to maintain good running form through the tape. He should aim to go through the 200 metres in a set time, and the first half of the race will be slightly faster than the second half.

Suggested training schedule for a 17-year-old schoolboy sprinter
Winter and Late Spring

Sunday	40 minutes fartlek.
Monday	Weight training.
Tuesday	300 metres in 42–5 seconds x 6 with a 5 minute jog recovery between runs.
Wednesday	20 minutes easy running.
Thursday	1. Weight training.
	2. Repetition uphill sprints.
Friday	
Saturday	200 metres x 3 (maximum effort), 200 metres jog recovery. 10 minute break.
	200 metres x 3 (maximum effort) 200 metres jog recovery.

Mid-May

Sunday 300 metres x 2 in 40 seconds with a 5 minute jog recovery.
7 minute break
150 metres x 4 in 19 seconds with a 3½ minute jog recovery.

Monday Weight training
20 minutes easy running on grass.

Tuesday 60 metre sprint starts from blocks x 6 with full recovery.
10 minute break
Up the clock session
100 metres almost flat out – 2½ minutes rest
120 metres almost flat out – 2½ minutes rest
140 metres almost flat out – 2½ minutes rest
160 metres almost flat out – 3 minutes rest
180 metres almost flat out – 3 minutes rest
200 metres flat out.

Wednesday ½ Weight training session
20 minutes easy running on grass.

Thursday 60 metre sprint start from blocks x 6 with full recovery.
150 metres bend running x 2 – flat out with full recovery. Play at other events.

Friday ———

Saturday Competition.

Late-June (i.e. close to peak season)

Sunday 30 minutes easy running on soft grass or at seaside.

Monday 150 metres x 4 (full effort) with 3½ minutes recovery.
10 minute break
300 metres x 2 (very fast stride) with 5 minutes recovery.

Tuesday ½ Weight training session
20 minutes easy running.

Wednesday	60 metres starts x 6 from blocks with adequate recovery.
	150 metres x 3 (flat out) with 5 minutes recovery.
Thursday	Easy jogging and comfortable fast striding on grass.
Friday	———
Saturday	Competition.

The schedules that are listed represent suggestions, for there can be almost as many schedules as athletes. It must also be noted that the change from the winter schedule to the summer schedule is a gradual and not an abrupt change, and that schedules are changed every two or three weeks.

7 The Hurdles

General background

All men's hurdle races involve 10 clearances.

The women's 100 metre hurdles race involves 10 clearances of the 3 ft. barriers.

Hurdling is primarily running at speed. Whilst the hurdles obviously necessitate a modification of running action, the interference of the hurdles with sprinting should be minimal. Whilst grace of movement is a characteristic of almost all top-class hurdlers, grace of movement alone is not enough. The prize is to the athlete who breasts the tape first and not necessarily to the athlete who appears technically the 'smoothest' over the barriers. The keynote of good hurdling is *effectiveness*. We need to help the hurdler to make an effective clearance and keep sprinting.

Qualities of the hurdler

The high hurdler should be a leggy sprinter. Most high hurdlers stand 6 feet tall. Shorter hurdlers usually have disproportionately long legs – they are 'Split to the ears'. The aspiring high hurdler who cannot sprint comfortably with a 3 stride pattern between the 3' 6" barriers should forget the event, for it is essential that the athlete's stride length fits in with the fixed 10 yard distance between the hurdles. The hurdler must also be supple about the hip joint in order to facilitate the technique of clearance. He must also be aggressive enough to attack the event and to withstand occasional contact with hurdles.

The 400 metres hurdler also needs speed, but requires rather more stamina than the high hurdler – he should be a useful per-former over 600 metres flat. Height and legginess are again an advantage, but are not a necessity, for the barriers are only 3' high.

Key features of high hurdling

Basic to the event is that the athlete appears to be sprinting. He should not appear to run and then jump the hurdle. This is obvious, and we must therefore ask.

'What must the athlete try to do in order to hurdle effectively?'

The answer is that the athlete must:
(a) Attack at the hurdle.
(b) Drive across the hurdle, extending powerfully from the rear leg.
(c) Think of a fast 'knee to chest' action of the lead leg. At the hurdle the athlete should think of lifting the knee rather than of lifting the foot.
(d) Bring the rear knee through late, fast and high. The rear knee then flows through into the stride away from the hurdle. The athlete does not need to think of 'lateness', for this will follow naturally from the effective execution of point (b)

FIG. 15. HIGH HURDLE CLEARANCE
(a) *Knee lift and* attack. (b) *Low position over hurdle.* (c) *Rear knee comes through high and athlete runs away from hurdle.* (*See also Plate 11*)

(e) Think of the arms contributing decisively. The lead arm is brought back as the athlete comes off the hurdle, coinciding with the rear leg action. The arms must also contribute during the running between hurdles, for the coach will stress running between hurdles as a vital phase of the event.

(f) Be 'all action' over the hurdles. There is no posed position over the hurdles. What the photographers show is a still of a position through which the athlete passes at speed.

Major fault 1:
Too high over hurdles.
   Correction:
   This may have been caused by the athlete having hit too many hurdles in the past, usually with the trailing knee or ankle.
   (a) Ensure adequate hip mobility.
   (b) Aim for greater dip at hurdles, for this facilitates the 'Bringing through' of the rear leg.
   (c) It may also help if the athlete pushes the head just a little further down as he takes the hurdle. He needs to look towards the bottom of the next hurdle.

Major fault 2:
Body too upright over the hurdle, usually followed by a jarred landing.

   Correction:
   Attack and dip.

Major fault 3:
Rear knee coming through too soon, pausing and not snapping through into the stride away from the landing. Again a jarred landing.

   Correction:
   Attack the hurdle, concentrating on rear leg extension at take-off, for this will prevent the rear knee from coming through too soon.

Then – zip the rear knee through, late, fast and high.

Major fault 4:
Lead leg off line (i.e. not in the line of run).

> *Correction:*
> (a) Check to ensure that the take-off is not too close (it should be about 2.30 metres away).
> (b) The athlete to think of lifting the knee in line with the line of run.

Major fault 5:
Feeble running between hurdles.
> *Correction:*
> (a) Check that the landing from the hurdle is not off balance.
> (b) Use arms, drive powerfully off hurdles and between hurdles.

Major fault 6:
General loss of form late in race.
> *Correction:*
> Fatigue? Ensure an adequacy of out-of-season stamina training, including abdominal work. Occasionally train over 7 hurdles rather than 4 or 5. Some training to be done when the athlete is tiring.

Major fault 7:
Athlete off-balance at the first hurdle.

> *Correction:*
> (a) Check stride pattern to the first hurdle. This is usually 8 strides, but might be 7 with a big hurdler. Occasionally you may need to change the starting leg and the number of strides to the first hurdle.
> (b) Possibly start a little closer to the line than with a normal sprint start in order that the 'normal' running position is achieved well before the first take-off.
> (c) More hurdle starts and *attack* – possibly with a soft-topped hurdle. Minor adjustments to stride length should normally be made to strides 4 and 5. To adjust the first 3

strides may spoil the start, whilst to adjust near the hurdle may disrupt the pattern of clearance.

400 metres hurdles

In the 400 metres hurdles there is less attack, less dip and less vigour of action over the hurdles than there is in the 110 metres high hurdles. Many of the technical points, however, remain the same, with the additional problem of fatigue during the later stages of the race.

FIG. 16.   CLEARANCE OF
INTERMEDIATE HURDLE

The 35 metres spacing between hurdles allows for flexibility of stride pattern. Some hurdlers might take 15 strides between hurdles all the way, whilst some might take 15 strides between hurdles until fatigue causes the stride length to be reduced: then they usually drop to a 17 stride pattern. Some hurdlers have been wise enough to cultivate the ability to hurdle from either foot, and may manage, say, a 14 stride pattern dropping to 15 strides. There are many acceptable variations in the stride pattern, the vital feature being that the hurdler appears to take the hurdles in his stride. The skill that the 400 metres hurdler must develop is the ability to make minor adjustments in stride pattern in order to take the hurdles comfortably. He needs to be able to do this in varying states of freshness and fatigue.

Many of the faults seen in the 400 metres hurdle race have been noted under the heading of 'High hurdles – Major fault – Correction'. Other faults are:

Major fault 1:
Inability to arrive at the correct take-off spot with comfortable running. This is usually seen as a chopped stride with loss of speed to the hurdle *and* the additional problem of using energy to pick up speed again after the hurdle clearance.

Correction:
(a) Ensure basic hurdling technique.

(b) Have the athlete running at hurdles (sometimes odd spacings) in different states of freshness and fatigue, so that small adjustments of stride length take place over, say, 20 metres and not during the final 10 metres to the hurdle.

Major fault 2:
Occasionally the above chopping (or, indeed, stretching the stride length to the hurdle) is caused by the athlete needing to put in an extra stride because he cannot hurdle from the 'wrong' leg.

Correction:
Hurdle from the wrong leg when fresh and when tired in order to acquire and consolidate technical efficiency. Do some hurdling with the hurdles at a 4 or 6 stride spacing.

Coaching positions for the hurdles events
The main coaching position is at right angles to the hurdle, some 15 metres from the hurdle. Almost all major faults will be observed from this point.

For the 'lead-leg in line' action, check for the fault with the athlete running towards the coach.

Suggested training schedules for

(a) 120 metres High hurdles
(b) 400 metres Intermediate hurdles.

Winter and late Spring
The basis of good technique must be laid during the winter months. The hurdler needs to take advantage of reasonable weather in order to hurdle outdoors twice a week if possible. He may also be able to do some hurdling indoors.

Interval running, resistance running, weight training and circuit training usually feature in the hurdler's winter training.

FIG. 17.   HURDLING EXERCISE

FIG. 18.   HURDLE EXERCISE

Flexibility is of primary importance to the hurdler. In the heavy events it is technique and strength that go hand in hand, but in the hurdles it is technique and mobility that are important. It is impossible to perform the intricate movements of hurdling unless the athlete is supple. Mobilising work, therefore, should be part of the hurdler's warm up routine for every training session.

	110 *metres Hurdles*	400 *metres Hurdles*
Sunday	150 metres × 6 with 3 minute recovery This is over 2′ 6″ hurdles spaced 20 metres apart. Repetition uphill sprints.	300 metres × 4 with a 3 minute recovery. This is over 4–6 hurdles at odd spacings. Repetition uphill sprints.
Monday	Weight training 20 minutes easy running.	Weight training 20 minutes easy running.
Tuesday	Fast runs over 4 hurdles, the hurdles to be set at a 3 stride spacing. Hurdle spaces adjusted to suit the athlete and the conditions —perhaps 8½ metres apart. Play at other events.	600 metres run × 2 (10 minute recovery) (hurdles at correct spacings, set only in final 200 metres). 200 metres sprints × 2 with a 200 jog recovery.
Wednesday	30 minute Fartlek: circuit training.	30 minutes Fartlek: circuit training.
Thursday	200 metres × 4 with 200 metres walk recovery. 10 minute break. 200 metres × 4 with 200 metres walk recovery.	
Friday	Weight training.	Weight training.
Saturday	—	Fartlek or Cross-country.

Training days can be rearranged to suit the athlete and the availablity of facilities. The above schedules are biased towards those athletes whose hurdling technique is relatively poor. Skilful hurdlers would often prefer a complete break from hurdling during the winter period.

Mid-May		
Sunday	Fartlek.	Fartlek.
Monday	Sprint runs over 7 hurdles × 6 with adequate recovery.	200 metres of intermediate hurdles × 3 with adequate recovery.
		10 minute break.
	Weight training.	200 metres run in 30 seconds, running on to final 200 metres with hurdles set up × 3 with 5 minute recovery.
Tuesday	150 metres very fast strides × 6 with 4 minute recovery.	Weight training.
		20 minutes easy running.
	'Play' at other events.	
Wednesday	20 minutes easy running.	300 metres run (with hurdles) × 3 with a 5 minute recovery.
	½ Weight training session.	150 metres flat × 3 with a 3 minute recovery.
Thursday	60 metres High Hurdles × 6 – as sprint start runs with an adequate recovery.	20 minutes easy running.
		½ Weight training session.
	100 metres flat out (from a rolling start) × 4 with a 3 minute recovery.	
Friday	—	—
Saturday	Competition.	Competition.
Late June		
Sunday	Fartlek.	Fartlek.
Monday	Sprint runs over 7 hurdles × 6 with adequate recovery.	As for Monday in mid-May.
	½ Weight training session.	
Tuesday	150 metres flat out × 4 with 5 minutes recovery.	½ Weight training session.
		20 minutes easy running.
	'Play' at other events.	
Wednesday	60 metres High hurdles × 4 with adequate recovery. Use a normal run in, with finishing posts.	300 metres run (with hurdles) × 2 with a 10 minute recovery.
		200 metres run (no hurdles) × 2 with a 5 minute recovery.
		100 metres run × 4 with a back recovery.
Thursday	20 minutes easy running.	30 minutes easy running.
Friday	—	—
Saturday	Competition.	Competition.

8 Middle Distance Running

General background
The middle distance events are:

800 metres
1500 metres, with the occasional 1 mile as a traditional event,
5000 metres
10000 metres

In the middle distance events the problems of the coach and athlete are less concerned with technique and more concerned with conditioning, both mental and physical.

Qualities of the Middle-distance runner
The middle distance runner is perhaps less concerned with natural physical attributes than athletes in other events. Obviously there are physiques that are completely unsuited to stamina running (fat people, for instance), but middle distance runners may be powerful, or wiry, or even quite weedy. Good middle distance runners, however, are endowed with certain mental attributes. They are prepared to persevere with their training over the years, and they are prepared to punish them-

selves in training. They are prepared to train under a variety of conditions, and they are prepared to train every day.

Key features of middle-distance running – Technical

The running action is 'toned down' from that of the sprinter. As the distance of the race increases there is less drive (both of legs and arms) and less knee lift. Fundamentally, the athlete needs to be able to relax at moderate speeds – he should appear to be running smoothly with relatively little effort.

Major fault 1:
Overstriding.
 Correction:
 Relax! The athlete must be able to accept more of a 'shuffling' gait, for this is economical.

Major fault 2:
Undue tension.
 Correction:
 (a) A high standard of fitness.
 (b) Confidence inspired by the coach.
 (c) A clear tactical plan.

Key features: tactical

Having established a sound physical condition, the athlete's main problem is to run the best race of which he is capable. This is to some extent dictated by his mental state. He should come to a race eager for success (and we must note the 'success' can be a personal best time in 8th place) and convinced that he is able to succeed. This may mean that the coach needs to limit the number of races to be run by the athlete, for a common fault of middle-distance runners is to over-race.

Major tactical problems include

1. The ability to judge pace. The athlete must be aware of pace during training, and must continually be able to assess the speed at which he is running, both when fresh and when tired. During training sessions the coach will often set the athlete to run a set distance in a certain time, and will then question the athlete as to the actual time of the run. Over the years the athlete will develop the ability to judge pace as a

result of continually needing to make judgements.

During races the athlete needs to be able to run at close to an even pace. What usually happens, for instance, in a mile race is that the athlete starts at a little faster than average pace, fades away a little during the third quarter and then speeds up again towards the end of the race. Nevertheless good races are run at close to even pace.

2. The ability to assess himself in the light of the running of other athletes. The athlete needs to decide what is best for him in the light of his own ability and that of the opposition. In the main this means:

(a) Keeping in touch with the leaders, preferably in 2nd or 3rd place.
(b) Avoiding being boxed in.
(c) Avoiding unnecessary chopping and changing of position.

3. As the athlete improves in ability and confidence he may feel the need to direct and dictate the race and employ more aggressive running tactics such as the 'surging' of Clarke or the fast bursts of Roelants.

Training for Middle-distance running – General points

1. Quantity precedes quality. Distance running during the winter precedes speed training during the summer. However, even during the winter period some attention must be paid to the *quality* of running, for distance alone is not enough.
2. The work load must be built up gradually.
3. Interval work must be sparingly used, and must be judiciously combined with other forms of training.
4. Days of intensive training should alternate with days of light training.
5. Variety is essential. This is achieved by:
   (a) changing the training schedule every two or three weeks.
   (b) coaching sessions which are 'surprise' sessions – i.e. which are not on the normal training schedule.

    (c) Occasional changes of venue and training companions. This might take the form of a day at the seaside with a long, easy run by a group of athletes followed by games. Or it might take the form of a 'paarlauf' competition in which pairs of athletes compete in a continuous relay for a set time or distance.

6. As the season approaches, some work must be done at racing speed and close to racing distance.

7. Peak season is for winning selected races. The aim is to produce what winter and spring have promised, and not to prove that hard training can lead to even harder training.

8. Competitions must be selected with care. Emotional, as well as physical condition must be carefully guarded.

9. Competitions must be seen in perspective. Some can simply be treated as part of the training programme, whereas others must be seen as being of vital importance. For these latter competitions the athlete must be prepared both physically and mentally for peak performance. Over-distance races (i.e. the 800 metre runner racing the occasional 1500 metres) may be taken as training during the early season period. The middle distance runner builds up his speed as the peak season approaches, combining his actual racing distance with the occasional under-distance event during the main racing season.

10. Training must be enjoyable!

Training Schedules for Middle-distance runners.

Definitions of fartlek, resistance running and interval running have been given in the section on 'Fitness Training', for some of this information is of value to all athletes. However the middle distance runner is concerned with the balance of various training methods, and particularly with the type and frequency of his *Interval training*.

Interval training
  Advantages:
    Economical of time.
    Physiologically efficient, imposing powerful stimulus upon

the heart and increasing the heart volume.

Can be *approximately* controlled and measured, and progress can be checked.

Disadvantages:

If applied unwisely, interval training can lead to staleness.
If used excessively, interval training may lead to injuries.
Frequent fast work on hard surfaces may lead to shin soreness, and possibly to a stress fracture.

The *basic plan* for runners is to aim to run

$\frac{1}{4}$ racing distance at slightly faster than racing speed x 8 with a 2 – 4 minutes rest period between efforts.

However this basic plan is varied in many ways, for there are four variables:

Distance of run

Speed of run

Length of interval

Number of repetitions.

The selection from these factors varies according to

(a) the event

(b) the ability of the performer

(c) the training period and its timing relative to the peak season.

In general, pre-season training will involve slow runs with a brief recovery. In-season training will progress to faster runs with a longer period of recovery: and to some work over a shorter distance.

Example

The basic pattern of training for an 800 metre runner aiming to run a 2 minute 800 metres might include (on one day of the week) interval training of the following type:

mid-March	200 metres in 32 seconds x 5–6 with a 200 metre fast jog recovery.
mid-April	200 metres in 32 seconds x 8 with a 200 metre fast jog recovery.
mid-May	200 metres in 30 seconds x 8 with a 200 metre jog recovery.
mid-June	200 metres in 29 seconds x 8 with a 200 metre slow jog recovery.

> 200 metres in 29 seconds x 4   with a 200 metre
> slow jog recovery.
>
> *July*   200 metres in 30 seconds x 8   with a 200 metre
> slow jog recovery.
>
> 200 metre flat out   x 1

Variations on interval running

1. *Increasing speed work-out.* (note the example given above of the training for the 800 metre runner in July)

2. *Tempo runs,* which involve very fast runs with a complete rest between efforts. This type of work is suitable for peak season training.

   Our 800 metre runner noted above might try a session which would be:

   300 metres at full speed x 4 with a 5 minutes rest between efforts.

3. *Interval work* based on the athlete's pulse rate rather than upon the judgement of the coach. The resting pulse rate of the athlete is generally in the region of 60 beats per minute. The coach must note, however, that this varies considerably between individuals. In working to maximum the athlete can probably push his pulse rate up to somewhere in the region of 180–200 beats per minute. This high pulse rate will drop rapidly, and the fittest athletes recover rapidly from a brief dose of intensive work.

   An interval session based on pulse count recovery might be (again for the 800 metre runner noted above):

   300 metres in 44 seconds x 4–6.

   The resting interval between runs would be the time required for the pulse rate to drop below 130 beats per minute. In all probability the coach would take a series of 6 second counts, sending the athlete off on each succeeding run when the pulse count fell to 13 beats in the 6 second period.

4. *Timed runs.* The athlete might run as far as possible in (say) 40 seconds and then take a 10 minute rest. On a

second run he would endeavour to beat the first distance. Sessions of this type are extremely tiring, and the coach would not expect the athlete to improve on a third attempt. For the third run, therefore, the coach would probably set a target which was some 10 metres *less* than the previous best effort. Training of this type would be a rare but interesting change from the regular training pattern.

5. *Differential runs.* A miler might run (say) repetition 400 metres in 62 seconds with the first 200 metres in 34 seconds and the second 200 metres in 28 seconds for the 62 second total.

A session of this type would be written down as

400 metres in 62 (34,28) x 6 with 400 slow jog recovery.

6. *'Up the Clock'* – used, in the main, by 400 and 800 metre runners. A first class 400 metre runner might, from a flying start, try:

110 metres in 12 seconds	4 minutes recovery
120 metres in 13.2 seconds	4 minutes recovery
130 metres in 14.4 seconds	4 minutes recovery
up to	
170 metres in 18.0 seconds.	

The above session would be a 'peak season' work-out, and, because of its intensity, be well removed from competition.

7. *'Up and down the Clock'*

8. *An acceleration session.* The athlete runs one distance and then, after a recovery jog runs a lesser distance at a greater speed.

A 4 minute 1500 metre runner in June might run:

800 metres in 2 min. 10 seconds with an 800 metres slow jog recovery

600 metres in 95 seconds with a 600 metres slow jog recovery

400 metres in 61 seconds with a 400 metres slow jog recovery

300 metres in 45 seconds with a 300 metres slow jog recovery

200 metres flat out.

With so many possible variations in interval training methods the coach is faced with considerable problems of selection! Probably the simplest rough guides are:

(a) Two sessions of interval training per week.
(b) A 'main thread' of training running from March to August, this main thread being based on the principle of:
$\frac{1}{4}$ racing distance x 8
(c) The second session each week to vary, but perhaps only two or three of the above variations to be used during any one season. Variety must be purposeful and not used merely for the sake of variety. It is always useful for the coach to have one interval training variation 'up his sleeve', to be used when he suspects the onset of staleness.

Here are suggested training schedules for a 17-year-old school-boy who aims to run 800 metres in 2 minutes in July. It is assumed that the athlete has a background of general winter fitness training, including some cross country running.

	March	mid-May	late June
Sunday	Steady 6 miles.	Steady 4 miles.	Steady 4 miles or day out at seaside or hills.
Monday	Differential 400 m runs. 400 m in 60 (32,28) × 4 with 400 m jog recovery.	200 m in 30 seconds × 8 with 200 m jog recovery.	200 m in 28.5 × 8 with 200 m very slow jog recovery.
Tuesday	Strength training. 20–30 minutes easy run.	Strength training. 20–30 minutes easy run.	Strength training. 20 minutes easy run.
Wednesday	200 m in 32 × 6 with 200 m fast jog recovery.	150 m in 20.5 × 4 with 250 m jog recovery. 10 minute break. 400 m in 56 seconds.	300 m in 42 × 2 with 500 m jog recovery 10 minute break. 150 m in 19 × 3 with 250m slow jog recovery.
Thursday	Strength training. 30 minutes steady run.	$\frac{1}{2}$ Strength training. 20 minutes steady run.	20 minutes easy run.
Friday	20 minutes easy run.	20 minutes easy run.	Jogging and striding only.
Saturday	Road Race or 600 m in 90 seconds: play at other events.	Race followed by repetition fast strides.	Race.

9 The Steeplechase

General background and qualities of the Steeplechaser
The 3,000 metres steeplechase event includes 7 water jumps and 28 clearances of hurdles 3 feet high. Towards the end of the race, when the athlete is tiring, these obstacles present a considerable problem. The steeplechaser, therefore, needs to face the stamina problems of the middle distance runner and the problem of reproducing skill in hurdle or water jump clearance. He also needs to be a resilient and tough runner, for the barriers involve change in pace and action.

FIG. 19.   STEEPLECHASE
Hurdle clearance

The young steeplechaser runs over distances of 1,500 metres and 2,000 metres, plans for these races are shown in the appendix.

FIG. 20.   STEEPLECHASE
*Water jump clearance. Pivot low over the
barrier and drive away*

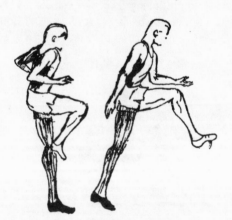

FIG. 21.   STEEPLECHASE
*Landing from water jump. Run
smoothly away from the landing*

Key features of hurdle clearance

1. As in the 400 metres hurdles except that there is
    (a) less dip and

(b) more relaxation and less snap.

2. Most important to be able to adjust running to the hurdle and to manoeuvre for a clear run at the hurdle.

Key features of Water Jump clearance

1. Acceleration to the barrier.
2. If a check mark is used, a clear run from the check mark to the barrier. The check mark is usually set some 7 running paces from the barrier. We must note, however, that there is a growing tendency for steeplechasers not to use a check mark, for the proliferation of athletes and check marks may mean difficulty in spotting a particular check mark.
3. Pivot and drive forwards and down from the barrier top, extending the rear leg powerfully.
4. Run away from the landing.

Safety at the Water Jump landing

It is important to have a landing with a little give and which is not muddy. An uneven or very hard landing is dangerous, and a muddy landing eventually becomes almost impossible to run out of. Many athletes prefer to land on an upturned fibre mat that has been firmly fixed.

Major fault 1:

As for the 400 metres, except that the steeplechaser would be unlikely to cultivate a 'wrong leg' lead.

Major fault 2:

Boxed in approach to hurdle or barrier.
   Correction:
   (a) run wide or
   (b) elbows out for a clear run to the hurdle or barrier.
The steeplechaser also needs to accelerate to the hurdle in order to prevent interference from the rear.

Major fault 3:

Failing to clear the water jump.

Correction:
(a) Concentrate on acceleration to the barrier and on staying low over the barrier.
(b) Pivot and then drive forwards and down from the barrier.

Major fault 4:
Stumbling on landing from the water jump.
    Correction:
    (a) Point (a) from 3 (above). Ensure that the athlete is not going too high over the barrier.
    (b) Ensure that the athlete has adequate leg strength and that he can endure the strain of landing.
    (c) Some barrier work in training.

Major fault 5:
Landing with both feet together off the water jump. Not running out of the water.
    Correction:
    (a) Keep the driving foot against the water jump rail for a slightly longer period of time.
    (b) Drive off the rail picking up the knee of the leading leg: hold this position fractionally.

Training for Steeplechasing
The arch enemy of the steeplechaser is fatigue. The differential between the time for 3,000 metres flat and 3,000 metres steeplechase is approximately 35 seconds for a competent athlete. It is generally thought that approximately half of this 35 seconds is due to barrier clearances and that the other half of this additional time is due to changes of pace and rhythm.

It follows that the prospective steeplechaser must be prepared for rigorous training programmes designed to develop a callous attitude towards tiredness and pain. It is hoped that this attitude will enable the athlete to maintain technical competence over both hurdles and water jumps even though he is in a state of fatigue.

Much of the young athlete's training will be done in the company of middle distance runners. This will include cross

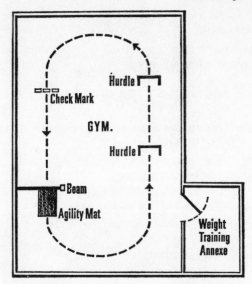

FIG. 22. INDOOR TRAINING
FOR STEEPLECHASE

country and resistance running, fartlek and interval running
on the track. Weight training is also necessary for most steeplechasers. One of the training problems that the novice will
encounter is the poor condition of water jumps during the
winter months. It is suggested, therefore, that one day per week
is spent indoors carrying out a skill training schedule on
hurdling and simulated water jump clearance. Where a reasonably large gymnasium is available the following procedure can
be adopted:

Winter Training Indoors

1. *Warm-up* (15 mins)
   Jogging-running-short sprints followed by mobility
   exercises including ground hurdling and hurdle stepping.

2. *Skill Practice* (20 mins)
   Circuits of the gymnasium taking the water jump and
   hurdles in each lap. Concentrate on good form over the
   obstacles.

3. *Weight Training* (30 mins)
4. *Skill Training* (10 mins)
    It is sometimes a good thing to repeat the skill practice when tired after weights.

Suggested training schedule for 17-year-old junior:

Winter

Monday	(a) Indoor Skill training as shown above.
	(b) Weight training.
Tuesday	4–5 miles Fartlek.
Wednesday	(a) Weight training.
	(b) 5 miles steady running.
Thursday	12 x 400 m (65) 400 m jog recovery.
	(a) Weight training.
Friday	4–5 miles Fartlek.
Saturday	Cross-Country.
Sunday	10 x 400 m with 5 hurdles (67–68) 400 m jog recovery

March

Monday	(a) Indoor skills.
	(b) Weight training.
Tuesday	10 x 400 m (63) 400 m jog.
Wednesday	(a) Weight training.
	(b) 5 miles Fartlek.
Thursday	6 x 800 m with 5 hurdles (2.24.0) 5 mins jog recovery.
Friday	(a) Weight training.
	(b) 5 miles steady running.
Saturday	Cross-Country.
Sunday	12 x 400 m with 5 hurdles (66) 400 m jog recovery.

Mid-May

Monday	8 x 200 m taking two hurdles and the water jump. Jog slowly for rest of lap to recover.
Tuesday	(a) 5 x 800 m (approx. 2.12.0) two laps jog recovery.
	(b) Weight training.
Wednesday	3 x 1200 metres with 5 hurdles (3.36.0) 10 mins recovery.

Thursday	(a) 6 x 200 m (fast) 200 m jog 90 secs. recovery.
	(b) ½ Weight training.
Friday	Rest.
Saturday	Competition.
Sunday	Fartlek (1 hour).

Late June

Monday	Fartlek (1 hour).
Tuesday	5 x 800 m with 5 hurdles (2.16.0) 7 mins recovery.
Wednesday	12 x 200 m (28) 200 m jog 90 secs. recovery.
Thursday	(a) Hurdling practice (20 mins).
	(b) 6 x 400 m (62) 400 m jog recovery.
Friday	Rest.
Saturday	*Competition.*
Sunday	Fartlek (1 hour) or hill running.

The times given in these schedules should only be used as a rough guide. The coach must work these out according to the capabilities and requirements of his athletes.

10 Relay Racing

(1) 4 x 100 METRES RELAY

General background
The sprint relay makes two simple demands upon the athletes:
(a) Excellence in sprinting
(b) Excellence in baton changing
Whilst both factors are vital, it is the latter factor of baton changing which can be improved quickly.

Each of the three baton changes must be made within a 20 metre zone. However, the outgoing runner may use an additional 10 metre zone before the 'change zone' in order to work up more speed. The race is run in lanes. What matters in relay racing is the speed of the baton round the track, and coaching is directed towards ensuring that this speed is always as close as possible to top running speed.

The recommended method of baton changing is that used by the national team which is
(a) non-visual
    and is
(b) a downward pass.
When the athlete has received the baton he keeps it in the receiving hand until he reaches the next runner. If a runner has the baton in his left hand he will pass it to the right hand of the next runner. Because of this the method of baton changing is known as the 'alternate' method.

The first runner assumes a normal crouch start with the baton in his right hand, the 2nd, 3rd and 4th fingers grasping the baton firmly. The first change is an inside change, being from the right hand of the first runner to the left hand of the second runner. The second change is an outside change and the final change an inside change.

FIG. 23.   WAITING FOR THE INCOMING RUNNER
4 x 100 metres relay

FIG. 24.   BATON CHANGE
*4 x 100 metres relay. Both runners at speed
and good 'free distance' at the change*

Whilst waiting for the change, the outgoing runner assumes a semi-crouch start position. As the incoming runner passes an agreed check mark, the outgoing runner drives away powerfully as in a sprint start. Some 12–15 metres from the start of his run the outgoing runner extends back the receiving arm, hand flat, palm uppermost with a 'V' between the thumb and forefinger. The outgoing runner continues to accelerate and also to keep a steady hand for the baton. The incoming runner drives in powerfully and passes the baton decisively into the palm of the outgoing runner. The exchange will probably take place at about the middle of the 20 metre zone. With a good change the following features are noted:

1. Both runners are moving at close to sprinting speed.
2. When the change occurs, there is good 'free distance' between the runners.

Establishment of the check mark

Initially this may be made some seven walking paces back from the beginning of the accelerating zone, the mark being made either with a scratch on the track surface or a sprinkling of talcum powder for clear sighting. The rule states: 'When a relay race is being run in lanes a competitor may place a check mark on the track within his own lane but may not place, or cause to be placed, any marking object on or alongside the track'.

This mark should be adjusted by practice between the two runners. The final measurement is made in foot lengths by placing the heel of one foot tight against the toes of the other. The total distance measured in this way generally works out between 26–34 foot lengths but, of course, will vary tremendously according to the length of the athlete's foot.

Key features of baton changing

1. Outgoing runner drives away powerfully, driving with legs and arms.
2. Outgoing runner extends back a hand which is high and steady.
3. Incoming runner drives in all the way and 'gives' decisively.
4. There is a gain of 'free distance' between the runners, i.e. the incoming runner succeeds in passing the baton but does not pass the outgoing runner.

Major fault 1:

Outgoing runner caught too soon.

---

12. The 800m Final at the Munich Olympic Games 1972. Left to right: Hoffmeister (DDR), Falck (Ger.), Sabaite (USSR), Zlateva (Bul.), Nickolic (Yug.), Silai (Roum.). Falck won in 1.58.6 and the first four beat 2.00 minutes, opening up a new era in women's 800m running. (*Tony Duffy*)
13. The Steeplechase at the Munich Olympic Games 1972. Biwott (Kenya) leads off the water jump. Jipcho (Kenya), 2nd from left, finished in 2nd position in the final behind Keino (Kenya) who won in 8.23.6 secs. (*Tony Duffy*)

(Photos: Tony Duffy)

Correction:

(a) Check to see that runner is driving away powerfully and is not just 'pattering' out.

(b) Ensure that outgoing runner's turn and start are simultaneous.

(c) If points (a) and (b) are not at fault, adjust the check mark.

Major fault 2:

Outgoing runner not caught, or has had to reduce speed towards end of zone.

Correction:

(a) Check that outgoing runner is not going too soon.

(b) Check that the incoming runner is not 'fading' at the end of his run. This may be caused by the incoming runner losing speed by running the last few strides with the baton arm extended. What he should do is 'drive' with the arms right up to the passing of the baton.

(c) If points (a) and (b) are not at fault, adjust the check mark.

Major fault 3:

Outgoing runner moving the receiving hand, making baton passing difficult for the incoming runner.

---

14. European Championships, Budapest, 1966, showing the second changeover in the 4 x 400 metres relay which was won by Poland (on extreme right). Borowski (496) has just handed over to Gredzinski (504).

Refer to page 100, which outlines the responsibilities of the outgoing runners on the second and third changes in the 4 x 400 metres relay. Here Poland and Germany (353 to 323) have succeeded in making good changes through being clear of the rest of the field. Martin Winbolt-Lewis (Gt. Britain) is receiving from John Sherwood, but is almost at a standstill owing to being hemmed in by Germany and France. Hungary are in a hopeless position, with Nemeshazi (706) looking for his partner Rabai (710) who is badly placed in lane 4 (second from left).

Of the other finalists, France and Italy are quite nicely placed, but Czechoslovakia and East Germany are not in good positions for efficient changes. No amount of practice between two men can entirely eliminate the chance of a poor baton exchange in the confusion caused by the jostling of 8 teams at this stage of the race. The main responsibility lies in the quick thinking and anticipation of the man who is to receive the baton (*Chapter 10*)

D

Correction:
(a) Check the hand position when the athlete is stationary. Have the runner extend arm and hand in front of him and then take the hand back and 'feel' the position. Then, as part of a sprinters' session on starting, practice starts with the hand going back some 12–15 metres from the start of his run.

The coaching position is from the side, perhaps 20 metres back from the estimated point of change. In training it is also useful to look from behind the outgoing runner in order to check fault (3) above.

The order of running. Various factors affect this

1. The first runner must be a good starter.
2. The 1st and 3rd runners need to be good 'bend runners'.
3. The 2nd and 3rd runners are involved in two baton changes, whereas the 1st and 4th runners are only involved in one change each.
4. The 4th runner must be reliable under stress.
5. The 1st runner may run a little more than 100 metres with the baton and the 4th runner may run a little less than 100 metres with the baton.

You pay your money and take your choice!

Organising the Coaching session
For sprinters, baton changing should be part of the weekly training programme from April onwards. It is also important to have at least 6 runners involved. Whilst the coach may have a good idea of his probable 4 runners for the Summer, it is as well to be prepared for injuries. It may also be that injuries will necessitate a change in the running order. Early season work, therefore, must cater for versatility, and each member of the team should be prepared to run in any position. Whilst the majority of practices will be based on an expected order of running, the coach must be prepared to accommodate mid-season injuries.

During a coaching session one coach cannot see all. What he should do, therefore, is to check the one or two most important features whilst other members of the team check other designated features. The coach should prepare stencils of 'check-off' sheets.

Check sheet for coaching 4 x 100 metres relay

Team: *Madeley College*

		Run number		
	Change no. 1	1	2	3
A.	*Incoming runner* K. L. Jackson			
	Driving all the way with the arms?	Yes	Yes	Yes
	Decisive 'give'?	Yes	Yes	Yes
	Fading in running?	No	No	Slightly
B.	*Outgoing runner* A. Yiannakis			
	Left as incoming runner hit check mark?	Early	Yes	Yes
	Maximum effort through zone?	Yes	Yes	Yes
	Hand back flat and high?	Yes	Yes	Yes
C.	Change took place at?	Failed	12m	18m
	(distance from start of *change* zone)			
	Change no. 2			
	etc.			
	Change no. 3			
	etc.			

Point (B) would probably be watched by the coach. Points (A) and (C) would be watched by other members of the team.

In all probability the coach would plan for perhaps two (if effective) or 3 changes between each pair. Then he would move on to another pair. He would probably work change (1), then change (3), then change (2). On the next training session, after a warm-up and a brief practice *organised by the team*, a full run might be tried with a check-off sheet being completed by other members of the club. Occasionally in training sessions the speed of the baton through the zone would be timed.

RELAY RACING (2) 4 x 400 METRES

The longer relay, although not run as often as the short sprint relay, has increased in popularity in recent years. Whilst baton changing is not as important as in the shorter race, it can represent a significant gain or loss. It is therefore important for teams to practice their baton changing.

The change generally employed is a non-visual change from the right hand of the incoming runner to the left hand of the outgoing runner. The change is an upward pass into the 'V' formed by the thumb and forefinger. The outgoing runner makes an early change of the baton from left hand to right hand, keeping a very firm grasp of the baton. Remember that there may be problems of fighting for the pole of the track.

The check mark used by the outgoing athlete is closer than

FIG. 25.   BATON CHANGE
4 x 400 metres relay

that used in the sprint relay, for the speed of the incoming runner is less. The outgoing runner estimates his speed away from the start on the basis of the speed of the incoming runner who may be 'dying' rapidly.

The first leg of the race is run in lanes and so is the first bend of the second leg. This creates problems of pace judgement, for the first runner will be running 400 metres on a 'stagger' made for 500 metres. Hence it is important for the first runner to have good pace judgement. The second runner may cut for the pole of the track (i.e. the inside lane) after the completion of the first bend of his run. The second and third baton changes take place within the same 20 metre zone but are not in lanes. Hence there may be movement and pushing on the start line as the incoming runners approach. At this stage it is the responsibility of the outgoing runner to position himself for the change. He needs to have taken his decision and be stationed when the incoming runner is still some 35 metres away. A tiring runner coming in cannot adjust as easily as a fresh runner on the line.

Order of running.

It is essential that the first man has a sound sense of pace judgement, and it is also essential that the last runner is a better than average performer with good pace judgement and tactical sense. A weaker man, who will fight if 'pulled through' by an opponent who leads, would usually be placed as number 2 or number 3 runner on the team.

Major fault 1:
Poor pace judgement when unhampered by other runners.
  Correction:
  Fast, controlled runs at speeds set by the coach, with some of this as solo work. Sessions in which the athlete runs and then estimates his time – the coach having held the watch.
Major fault 2:
Poor pace judgement when in contact with other runners.
  Correction:
  Athlete to run his *own* race. A great weakness in the 4 x 400 metres relay is for a runner to start his leg in arrears and then to try to recoup his team's loss too soon. In all probability he will then fade very badly at the end of the race.
  The fault may also be apparent when an athlete starts his leg in the lead and 'loafs' round the track – fatal against someone with better basic speed.
Major fault 3:
Mix-up at baton change.
  Correction:
  There must be a clear apportionment of responsibility. The incoming runner must try to drive in and maintain good running form and the outgoing runner must position himself for the baton change.
  The coach should plan for some baton changing work for his team when 3 or 4 changes are made almost simultaneously. In order to be prepared for possible barging during the race, barging during training must be simulated.

11 Race Walking

General background

The Race Walking Association defines walking as a
'progression by steps so that unbroken contact with the
ground is maintained.'

This means that the advancing foot must make contact with
the ground before the rear foot leaves the ground.

The A.A.A. provide track championships over 3000 metres
and 10,000 metres, the W.A.A.A. over 5000 metres. There are
also track championships for A.A.A. Youths and W.A.A.A.
Intermediates and Juniors over suitable distances.

The R.W.A. hold championships over the following distances:
10 miles, 20 miles, 20 kilometres and 50 kilometres. In the major
international championships races are held over 20 kilometres
and 50 kilometres.

Race walking is now being increasingly introduced into the
schools. In some cases the youngsters who are good 'all-
rounders' are succeeding, whilst in other cases it is the boys who
can achieve little at other sports who do well.

Qualities of the walker

In the first instance any boy who is encouraged and guided
by the teacher or coach can take part in and enjoy walking.
This will increase the youngster's general state of fitness. Long
walks and hikes make occasional out of season training variations for athletes from a number of events. At the level of good
class competition, however, race walkers are characterised by
qualities of fitness, willingness to train under adverse conditions

and perseverance.

Key features of Race Walking
  (a) *Body carriage*
       The trunk should be held comfortably erect. Forward
       lean should never be more than 5 degrees as it will pre-
       vent correct hip swing by limiting the forward thrust.
       Backward lean throws strain on the back muscles and
       again limits the hip swing. The head should be erect on
       the shoulders and the whole upper body have the feeling
       of sitting comfortably on the pelvis.
  (b) *Use of the hips*
       As in running by pushing the hip forward, with the leg
       an increase in stride length can be obtained. This will
       bring each foot on to a single line of direction providing
       a full hip thrust has been obtained. Fluent use of the
       hips is vital to good walking. The athlete should reach
       in a downward direction with the thrusting hip and bring
       the hip of the trailing leg through low. By this he will
       contact the ground more quickly. The hips perform a
       paddling movement, with hip of the recovering leg
       dropped as the feet pass.
  (C) *Legs*
       The recovery (trailing) leg must be bent as it comes
       through with the dropped hip. It then straightens to
       make contact with the ground heel first. Shortly after
       contact it first levers the body forward and then thrusts
       to full stride. The feet should pass each other closely
       and the rear leg remain locked until it leaves the ground.

  (d) *Feet*
       The toes should be carried slightly outward when pass-
       ing. The foot should make contact with the ground heel
       first then outside of the foot, ball of the foot and finally
       big toe joint.

  (e) *Arms and Shoulders*
       The arms are used merely as balancers. They should be
       bent at the elbows hands loosely clenched and move

slightly across from a point behind the hip to the centre line of the body. The shoulders should be kept down. If they rise they tend to make the walker lift and break contact.

Major faults 1:
Head Bobbing
Body lifting and lowering
   Correction:
   Caused by incomplete hip movement. Work on hip thrust and mobility.

Major fault 2:
Stride too short in front of body
(The rear leg breaks too soon in a quick action with a high knee lift).
   Correction:
   The stride should be extended and work carried out on hip movement. Better use of arms also helps.

Major fault 3:

Constantly bent knees
   Correction:
   Should be stopped immediately even when within the definition of walking. Ground hurdling exercises will assist using hands for pressure on knees to keep them straight. Constant correction is required by coach in order to alter this technique.

Major fault 4:
Shoulders lifting high
(Doubtful contact with ground).

   Correction:
   1. Upper body should ride easily on the pelvis.
   2. Consciously drop the shoulders and work to obtain an easier and more fluent arm action.

Major fault 5:
Side dip on shoulders
(Accompanied by side to side hip swing).

Correction:

Caused by exaggerated hip action.
1. Steady the shoulders.
2. Aim at a more direct forward hip thrust.

Major fault 6:
Foot pauses before reaching the ground
Correction:
When not caused by overstriding should be corrected by:

1. Better hip action.
2. Reaching for ground with the hip.
3. Keeping the rear foot on the ground for longer.

Walking Distances
Broadly speaking walking is divided into Track and Road. Specialisation takes place on a wide basis:

(a) 1–10 miles (sprint events).
(b) 10–20 miles (middle distance events)
(c) 20–50 miles (long distance events).

Races of one mile distance on the track and 3 miles on the road are recommended for schools.

The majority of 7–10 mile events take place in the winter and the 1–7 miles events in the summer.

Training schedules for walking events
Since the walker requires strength, mobility, skill and endurance it follows that supplementary training should be included in the programme. Weight training, circuit training and mobility exercises should be used according to the needs of the individual. However, since the skill of race walking is of primary importance a large proportion of time should be devoted to technique work. It is advisable to have a coach present, especially in the early stages of a walker's training to

ensure that contact is being maintained and good form adhered to during the exercise. When he becomes more experienced he should be able to know himself whether things are going well or not.

Warming-up

Walking to a slow rhythm for a few laps followed by further laps putting in bursts of speed over 30 to 40 m. Concentrate on some points of technique during this period. Loosening and suppling exercises should follow, the whole taking about 20–25 mins.

Number and duration of sessions per week

Three to five training sessions per week are found to be sufficient for the young walker. Environment, mental attitude, general strength and recovery rate must be taken into consideration when setting the schedule for any one athlete. Since distances vary in competition from 1 mile for juniors to 50 kilometres for seniors, so will schedules differ tremendously in their construction.

Strolling for sprint walkers

Strolling between 4–5 miles per hour is an essential part of the Walker's technique work to improve the hip action. A rough guide as to time and distance in the sessions will be 1 hour for 1 mile events, and up to 3 hours for the 7–10 mile events. The shorter the time allocated the faster the walk should be. Occasionally faster strolls should take place up to 6 miles per hour.

Training for the Road Events

Little track work is carried out and most of the training takes place on the roads. It is recommended to work out in graded packs according to ability.

These longer distances are not recommended for the school-boys. When he gets older and stronger and wishes to take part in middle and long distance road races he should be guided by his club as to the type of training he should undertake.

Feet and footwear

Care of the feet, as with the distance runner, is an all-important factor in Race Walking. Light shoes with leather uppers and a 3/8 inch microcellular heel with dye-free woollen socks will ensure maximum comfort and protection. Keep the feet clean by washing in tepid water and drying carefully. Hard skin should be removed by scraping not cutting.

12 The Throwing Events
Shot Put: Javelin Throw: Discus Throw: Hammer Throw

The Fundamentals of Throwing

The aim of the thrower is to throw as far as possible. He must do this within the framework of the rules, and these will involve staying within a defined area until the throw is acknowledged as being valid.

In order to throw as far as possible, the thrower must meet two major technical requirements.

1. To throw at the optimum angle of release.
2. To release the implement with maximum velocity, which involves:
   (a) The application of force through the greatest possible range.
   (b) The use of the strongest muscles to best advantage – in particular, the use of the legs.
   (c) The summation of all possible forces.
   (d) Working at speed.
   (e) Enough strength to perform the technical requirements of the event.

Qualities of the Thrower

Top class throwers are almost invariably fast, strong and agile. They are competent sprinters over a short distance (say, 40 metres) and competent weight lifters. They are often posssessed of considerable mobility and range of movement. They are aggressive in their throwing and they are prepared to work hard over the years in order to master the complications of throwing technique.

General points concerning the coaching of the Throws

Unless an athlete is possessed of the above physical qualities he will not make a top class thrower. However, athletes who are not well endowed physically can still hope to achieve a fair degree of success at domestic level as a result of careful application over a number of years, particularly in an event in which national standards are low.

The point has already been made that if the coach is doubtful about the reason(s) for a technical fault at one stage of an event then he should look again ...

'That's fine: now let's see another three puts'

... the coach should possibly look at the preceding stage of the event. Faults occur for a number of reasons, and faults often occur in the throwing events as a result of the physical limitations of the athlete. The detection of faults is often extremely difficult in the throwing events. If in doubt, *the coach should look at the feet*, for the footwork will often provide a clue to the origin of a particular fault.

Note: In the following descriptions it is assumed that the thrower is right handed.

SHOT PUT

General principles

The shot put, like the javelin throw, is an 'on-line' event. The athlete must endeavour to apply force along a straight line.

Once the athlete starts the implement moving then he must keep it moving forwards and forwards-upwards at increasing speed, aiming to achieve maximum speed at release.

As a general rule he must

'Keep it going forwards and then hit it late and fast.'

Basically the shot put can be thought of as a 'shift and lift' – a rapid shift across the circle followed by a powerful lift from the rear leg.

The accepted method of putting is the 'O'Brien' or 'back-facing' method. This, amongst other things, enables the athlete to be in contact with the shot through a greater range than would have been possible in the old 'side-facing' method of shot putting.

The starting position is one in which the athlete is looking back and the left hand and the feet are pointing back. The shot is touching the chin and neck and is held on the fingers rather than in the palm. The shot putter should conclude the competition with a clean palm and a dirty neck!

From this starting position, the key features of good shot putting are:

1. Movement across the circle is low and fast. The rear leg extends and the swing of the left leg towards the front of the circle contributes to speed across the circle. The right foot 'slurs' across to land in the centre of the circle.

2. There is no stopping in the front of the circle. The 'putting position' is a position through which the athlete passes and not a position in which he pauses.

3. There is tremendous *lift* from the rear leg, and a complete extension of the body as the put is made.

A.

B.

FIG. 26. SHOT PUT
(*a*) *Stay low, drive across the circle, keep looking back.* (*b*) Lift *from the rear leg*

The athlete should remember to:

(a) Drive across the circle, low and fast.
(b) Keep looking back.
(c) *Lift* from the rear leg.

Coaching positions

1. At side, some 15 metres back from the athlete: check
   (a) Drive across circle – extension of rear leg.
   (b) Is the backward lean of the body maintained across the circle?
   (c) Does the right foot land on the centre of the circle?
   (d) Is there continuity from the 'shift' to the 'lift'?
   (e) Is there a powerful lift from the right (rear) leg?
2. From behind the athlete, some 10 metres back: check
   (a) Is the back-facing position maintained as the athlete moves across the circle?
   (b) Where does the left foot land at the front of the circle relative to the line of put?
   It *should* be slightly to the athlete's left as he turns to put. If the left foot is in line with the line of put it will prevent the athlete from bringing his right hip through effectively into the 'lift'. If the left foot is too much to the left it means that he has turned too much to the front of the circle and that the final rapid lift and turn is through a shorter range of movement. In this latter position (i.e. the left foot too much to the athlete's left) the foot is stated to be 'in the bucket'.

Major fault 1:
Early loss of back-facing position, resulting in poor use of legs. The athlete appears to be working early with the throwing arm and to little effect.
Correction:
(a) Ensure correct alignment of feet (pointing back) before the start of the movement across the circle.
(b) Have the athlete look back at a fixed object, and keep looking back as he crosses the circle.
(c) Think of keeping the left hand pointing back.
(d) (or) Maintain the alignment of the right shoulder in the movement across the circle.
(e) Check that the left foot is not 'in the bucket'.
It is probably wise for the coach to limit himself to suggesting up to two of these corrections in any one coaching session.

Major fault 2:
Loss of back lean in movement across circle.
   Correction:
   Think of a faster right foot.

Major fault 3:
Pausing in the middle of the circle... possibly 'settling' (i.e. bending the right leg) before the put.
   Correction:
   (a) Ensure the the athlete *is* landing on a bent right leg.
   (b) Avoid too much work on standing puts. The coach must stress continuity and should only rarely put the athlete working on standing puts.
   (c) Ensure that the athlete is strong enough to work effectively from the ideal low position in the front of the circle.

Major fault 4:
Throwing the shot, usually caused by dropping the elbow and taking the shot away from the neck.
   Correction:
   Elbow *up*, keep the shot into the neck.

Major fault 5:
Ineffective lift from right leg.
   Correction:
   (a) Check that leg foot is not 'blocking'.
   (b) Consciously lift up with the right hip and extend the right leg.

Major fault 6:
A low put with the athlete falling off to his left.
   Correction:
   (a) Rear leg extension.
   (b) Keep left shoulder up for slightly longer, look up at 40 degrees plus. (Put should be in the region of 43 degree angle of release).

JAVELIN THROW
General principles
   The javelin thrower, unlike other throwers, has the advantage

of being able to take a lengthy run. However, herein lies a danger: a long run is of little value if the athlete runs, slows down considerably and then throws. Ideally the event comes close to being a running throw – it should *not* be a run *followed* by a throw.

In the idea of a running throw, however, the athlete faces a problem in that he wishes to use the speed of his approach run to best advantage, but that he also needs what is a contradiction to running speed – a wide firm base from which he can drive effectively. Hence the javelin thrower should run into a good throwing position. He should also work early and powerfully with the right leg (he lifts late with the left leg), and should bring in the arm late and fast.

Characteristics of a good throw

Although there are a number of methods by which the athlete can hold the javelin, the recommended method is the 'V' grip in which the javelin is held on the palm, between the first and second fingers. The length of the approach run varies, but it is usually in the region of 13 strides. During the initial part of the run the javelin is carried over the shoulder. It is withdrawn into the throwing position (of the arm) some 5 strides before the throw and is aligned with the line of throw 2 strides later. The approach run is well balanced and is made at the greatest speed that the athlete can control. The athlete runs into the throwing position, driving from the left foot and bringing the right knee through fairly high. As the athlete arrives in the throwing position the hips are to the front and the shoulders are still to the side. From the throwing position the right leg drives the body weight quickly forwards. The left leg bends a little and then straight just before the throw is completed. At this stage the head is turned to the left.

Key features of javelin throwing for athlete to think about
1. Maintaining speed and driving (especially from the left foot) in the throwing position.
2. A wide (greater than one's height) throwing base with the javelin left well behind.

    'Run away from the javelin.'

FIG. 27.   JAVELIN
*Left shoulder whipped round, right heel turned and
hip into the throw (This follows on action shown
in Plate 17)*

3. Landing heels first, feet pointing slightly to the right.
4. Getting the hip into the throw – driving the right hip to
   the front. *Initiate* this movement by 'whipping round' the
   right heel.
5. Keeping the right hand high.
6. Throw over a braced left leg.

Coaching positions
  1. From behind the athlete. check
     (a) Is the javelin 'on line'?
  2. From the side, some 15 metres back from the athlete and
     at right angles to the throw: check
     (a) Does the athlete leave the javelin well behind as he goes
         into the throwing position?
     (b) Is there a premature bending of the throwing arm?
     (c) Does the athlete maintain speed into the throwing
         position?
     (d) Does the athlete move through the throwing position,
         or does he 'settle' in it?

(e) Has he a wide throwing base?
(f) Does he work with the right hip?

In general, we need to ask ourselves
'Does the athlete work through the full range of movement?'
The wide throwing base and the right arm left well behind
will contribute to this. The athlete will also aim to get the feet
ahead of the javelin as he runs into the throwing position, for
this will help him to achieve a little 'back lean' and further
increase the range through which force is applied to the javelin.

More than in any other event, *some* faults stem from the
use of unsuitable equipment. The javelin thrower should wear
javelin boots, throw from a runway that is firm, and should
throw a javelin that is designed for effective throwing. In a
book which is aimed at club coaching it would perhaps be
wrong to deal with the aerodynamic problems of javelins. However it must be noted that an airborne javelin possesses co-
efficients of lift and drag, and that in a well designed javelin the
$\frac{\text{coefficient of lift}}{\text{coefficient of drag}}$ is high. Sufficient also to note that research
has proved that some javelins can be thrown farther than other
javelins! A considerable amount of research has gone into the
reproduction of the 'Held' javelin, and it is this type that is
recommended. 'Held' javelins have been designed for throws
in a certain distance range, so that (for instance) an athlete can
select a '70 metre' javelin.

We must also note the general problem in the throwing
events, which is the problem of skill breakdown. In striving for
a better throw the athlete increases speed to the point at which
the skill is lost, for he is not able to co-ordinate the appropriate
movements at that speed. The best throws inevitably come
when the athlete is working as fast as possible with control –
and these throws feel easy. One of the athlete's aims in training
for a throwing event is to push back the skill breakdown barrier
to the point at which he is working at speed *and* retaining the
skill of the event.

Major fault 1:
Running – standing still – and then throwing.

Correction:
Throw from a short approach run, stressing the continuity of the throw and of working early with the right hip. Then gradually increase the length and speed of the approach run Whilst maintaining control.

Major fault 2:
'Settling' in the throwing position.

Correction:
Avoid bounding into the throwing position – aim to run in low and then work early with the right hip. Right foot to land heel first.

Major fault 3:
Failure to drive the right hip into the throw.

Correction:
(a) Ensure that the throwing base is sufficiently wide.
(b) Ensure that the left foot is very slightly off to the thrower's left.
(c) Initiate hip thrust from right heel whip. Drive in from the left foot, bringing the right foot through quickly.

Major fault 4:
Considerable loss of speed as the thrower runs into the throwing position.

Major fault 5:
An 'off line' throw, caused by pointing the javelin out to the right as the athlete runs into the throwing position.

Correction:
(a) Check that the grip is correct. ('V').
(b) Keep the palm upwards.
(c) Feel that the javelin point is over the head as the throw is made.

Major fault 6:
A 'bent-arm' throw, caused by anticipating the throwing action of the arm.

Correction:
Athlete to leave the throwing arm behind as he runs into the throwing position. He should feel that he is 'running away' from the javelin.

Major fault 7:
Excessive javelin vibration in flight.
Correction:
Ensure that the force is applied in the line of throwing and that the athlete is not dragging down the hand just before release.

Major fault 8:
Javelin angled too steeply and then 'stalling'.

Correction:
Keep the palm a little higher and the point a little lower just before the release. Note that the angle of release will depend upon the type of javelin. The 'Held' javelins should be released in the 25 degree range whereas the older type of javelin would necessitate a release at a greater angle.

Major fault 9:
Point not coming down – no mark is made, and hence there is a 'No throw'.

Correction:
(a) As for point (8) above.
(b) Check that the 'Held' thrower is using the correct javelin for his distance of throw.

Major fault 10:
The injury of 'Javelin elbow'.

Correction:
(a) Ensure that the 'V' grip is used.
(b) Have the athlete think of the javelin coming 'over the top' rather than 'round the side' of the body.

Major fault 11:
Excessive falling away to left just before the throw is made.

Correction:
(a) Ensure adequate strength of left leg.
(b) Throw over a braced left leg.
Note that the final straightening of the left leg from this braced position may add to the throw.

Major fault 12:
A sluggish arm action into the throw.
Correction:
Just before the right arm is due to work, open the chest by swinging the left arm (i.e. elbow) outwards. This must be an aggressive movement.

DISCUS THROW
General principles
The general principles of forward movement, initial use of the strongest muscles followed by the use of faster arms movements applicable in the javelin and shot are equally applicable in the discus throw. In the case of the discus throw, however, the athlete's solution to the problem of a circle is to turn in it. Whilst the athlete runs forward to generate speed he also rotates in the circle. Indeed the accepted form of the throw is known as the 'running rotation'. This running rotation technique aims to get the athlete into a sound 'standing throw' position with the discus having more speed than a standing throw would allow, and with the athlete well ahead of the discus. Again we must note that the throwing position is a position through which the athlete passes at speed and is not a position in which the athlete pauses. One further point is that the 'running rotation' technique enables the feet to get ahead of the discus and a torque effect to be achieved. This means that the discus comes through late and fast. In order to be able to achieve this position well head of the discus the athlete must be flexible, for there must be adequate hip/shoulder displacement.

Characteristics of a good throw
The athlete starts with a 'back-facing' technique – i.e. away from the direction of throw. The turn is made through 450 degrees. The athlete's position is relaxed, the knees bent and

the feet some 40–50 cm apart. After two or three preliminary swings the thrower takes the weight decisively over the ball of the left foot and drives forwards across the circle. The right foot follows, low and fast to the centre of the circle, the thrower landing on a bent right leg. Some athletes prefer to think of a high right knee (as in a sprint) as the movement across the

FIG. 28.   DISCUS
*Land on a bent right leg
with the discus left well
behind*

FIG. 29.
Lift *into the throw*

circle is made: other athletes dispense with the high right knee and think of a fast right foot. The throwing position is established when the left foot lands at the front of the circle, slightly to the left of the line of throw. It is important that the left foot is down quickly in order to establish a firm throwing base. Now the right leg works powerfully, lifting . . . finally the arm comes in late and fast.

Key features of Discus throwing for the athlete to think about:
1. (At the commencement of the turn) Weight decisively over the ball of the left foot, keeping the left heel low and showing a 'bandy' position of the knees: then drive from the left foot.
2. A fast right foot, getting the body ahead of the discus.
3. Keeping the discus high.
4. Left foot fast to the front of the circle.
5. Lifting powerfully from the right leg, over a braced left leg.

Coaching positions
1. *From the rear* (so that the athlete is throwing away from you), check
   (a) Is the weight over the left foot as the athlete goes into the turn?
   (b) Does the athlete drive from the left foot?
   (c) Does the right foot move quickly to the centre of the circle?
   (d) Is the left foot off line in the front of the circle?
   (e) Position ahead of discus and height of discus during turn.
2. *From the 'open' side* Note: Whilst the 'open' side (i.e. the thrower's chest faces the coach just before the throw is made) is clearly the better side for seeing what happens in the throw, it may be dangerous to coach from this side if protective netting is not situated between coach and athlete. Check
   (a) Forward lean and drive across the circle.
   (b) Position ahead of the discus.
   (c) The throwing position and the drive up from the right leg.

(d) The release at shoulder height.

(e) The alignment of the shoulders just before release – in particular note that the left shoulder is not dropped.

Major fault 1:

Into the turn:

Falling off balance.

> *Correction:*
> Work decisively off the ball of the left foot, and think of running into the turn rather than spinning.

Major fault 2:

Jumping up into the turn.

> *Correction:*
> Start low, stay low, fast right foot.

Major fault 3:

Losing the position ahead of the discus.

> *Correction:*
> (a) As for (2) above.
> (b) Leave the discus behind as the turn is started.

Major fault 4:

Landing off balance in the centre of the circle.

> *Correction:*
> (a) As for (1) above.
> (b) *Or* be quite certain that the athlete is ready for the 450 degree turn. With novice athletes it is advisable to work through only 360 degress for the first season. In preparation for the second season the athlete will gradually increase his working range – i.e. to perhaps 400 degrees and eventually up to 450 degrees.

Major fault 5:

'Settling' in the front of the circle

> *Correction:*
> As for (2) above.

Major fault 6:

'Scooping' the discus.

The Throw:

Correction:
Use a horizontal preliminary swing(s). Go into the turn with the discus at or above waist height.

Major fault 7:
Losing a good torque position by 'waiting' in the front of the circle.
Correction:
Low turn and strike earlier with the right leg.

Major fault 8:
Discus going off right in throw, athlete falling off to left.
Correction:
(a) Keep the left shoulder up during throw.
(b) Easy throws, thinking of pushing the left foot slightly out to the left.
(c) Ensure that athlete is not 'blocking' with left foot.

Major fault 9:
Reversing too early, i.e. before the throw has been completed.
Correction:
The coach must be quite sure that there is a fault. If the athlete has worked effectively and at speed, then he may find that the right foot is off the ground just before the discus has been released. This is perhaps the result of rapid movements and may not be a fault.

If, however the right foot is off the ground *before* effective work has been done then it is a fault. The correction is to think of the right leg extension and of pushing the right toe back into the ground.

Major fault 10:
Falling out of the front of the circle.
Correction:
(a) Check that forward movement across the circle is not too great, and that the athlete is not crowding the front of the circle in his throwing position.
(b) Check that the left leg is being braced.
(c) Drop the body weight low immediately after the throw.

HAMMER

General principles

Whilst the discus thrower is concerned with turning and running forward in the circle, the hammer thrower is primarily concerned with turning. He does move forward across the circle as a result of his footwork, for each turn involves the thrower moving forward for two foot lengths. Most throwers use 3 turns and this is the technique that we shall consider. Some throwers use 4 turns, and this modification of technique involves changed footwork on the first turn in order to travel a shorter distance across the circle.

Most throwers turn in an anti-clockwise direction. The hammer handle is held with the left hand underneath the right hand, and the thrower will wear a protective glove (designed for the purpose) on the left hand. After two or three preliminary swings of the hammer round the head (using the maximum range of movement) the thrower commences the turn. The turning action is: heel – side of the foot – ball, and this action is the basis of good hammer throwing.

The aims of the hammer thrower are:

(a) To have the hammer as far as possible from the thrower – i.e. to have the longest possible radius of swing.

(b) To turn at increasing speeds, culminating into maximum velocity at the end of the final turn when the athlete lifts with the legs just prior to release.

The speed of turning is not an even speed. The thrower aims to accelerate into the turn so that the hips get ahead of the shoulders and the shoulders are ahead of the hammer. The hammer head is accelerated during its downward swing. The athlete pauses fractionally on a stable base (bent knees) and allows the hammer *almost* to catch him up. He then accelerates into the next turn, imparting even greater speed to the hammer head with each turn.

Key features of hammer throwing

1. Wide radius of preliminary swings.
2. Correct 'heel – side of foot – ball of foot' action during turns.

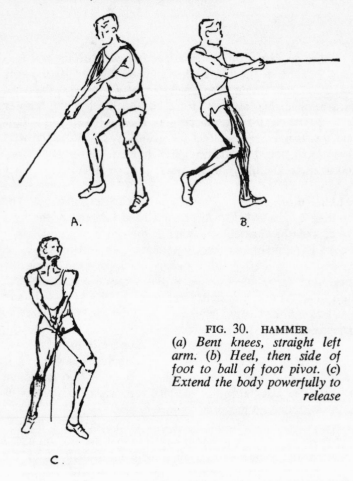

FIG. 30. HAMMER
(a) *Bent knees, straight left arm.* (b) *Heel, then side of foot to ball of foot pivot.* (c) *Extend the body powerfully to release*

3. Bent knees and *slight* back lean to counterbalance and control the centrifugal pull of the hammer.
4. Left arm straight, right arm almost straight.
5. Acceleration from turn to turn, with each turn starting fractionally earlier than the previous turn. This means that the low point of the hammer, relative to the position of the right foot, moves slightly back – i.e. in a clockwise direction.
6. An extension of the body at the end of the final turn.

Athletes should think about:
1. Footwork (but not to look at the feet – that is the coach's task!)
2. Maintaining the bent knee position, and feeling a controlled position between the turns.
3. Straight arms (push the elbows together).
4. Lifting into the throw.

Coaching positions
1. *From the rear,* check:
   (a) Radius of preliminary swings.
   (b) Footwork progressing in a straight line, and the feet coming progressively closer at the end of each turn.
   (c) The position of the hammer when the turn commences, noting that with each turn it should move progressively back.

2. *From the side,* check:
   (a) Bent knee position between throws.
   (b) The turning action of the left foot, and the path of the right foot which should be low and close to the left foot.
   (c) The increasing speed of turning of the left foot into the turns, and in particular a fast left foot into the final turn.
   (b) Straight arms.
   (e) The maintenance of ground contact, i.e. not jumping into the turns.

Major fault 1:
Too slow into 1st turn.
   Correction:
   Work more aggressively, and for a greater range, in the preliminary swings.

Major fault 2:
Bent arms – caused by the thrower feeling that he cannot withstand the pull of the hammer.

Correction:
Check the feet and the posture – is the athlete able to with-stand the pull? He might need to
(a) concentrate on bent knees
(b) then push the elbows together.

Major fault 3:
Inability to move across the circle in a straight line.
Correction:
Concentrate on footwork without any concern as to the distance thrown. Practice 5 or 6 turns from concrete slab, i.e. not using circle.
Ensure that footwork is low.

Major fault 4:
Leaving the ground during the turns, usually as the speed increases.
Correction:
(a) Greater knee bend.
(b) Improved footwork.

Major fault 5:
No acceleration after the 2nd or 3rd turn, possibly because the athlete has reached the limit of his control.
Correction:
(a) Start less quickly and aim to build up speed rather than hitting top speed too soon.
(b) Think of a faster left foot into the turn and then a firm base between the turns.

Major fault 6:
Lack of balance in the turns.
Correction:
(a) More practice on turns.
(b) Check head position – some athletes, in their striving for correct footwork, make the mistake of looking at their feet.

Major fault 7:
Anticipating the release and working with the arms.

Correction:
The use of the arms at release is only incidental: the athlete should work with the legs.

Major fault 8:
No lift at release.
Correction:
Check for bent knee position and that athlete is far enough ahead of the hammer: then coach for leg lift.

Major fault 9:
Falling out of circle.
Correction:
Check footwork across circle: then coach for lowering of weight after release.

TRAINING FOR THE THROWS

General fitness preceded specific fitness, and the thrower must remember that he is an athlete before he is a thrower. The thrower can and should benefit from some running training. This might take the form of fartlek during the winter, some interval running during the spring and sprints during the summer. The thrower might also play, say, Basketball during the winter and might participate in other throwing events and in jumping events during the summer.

Technique work, for the young thrower, should be carried on for at least 10 months of the year. An experienced thrower will probably take a longish break from throwing during the winter, possibly as much as 4 months.

Strength work goes hand in hand with technique work, for the skill of throwing may change slightly as the athlete increases in strength. The thrower would normally weight train some 3 times a week in the winter and spring, reducing to twice a week during the summer.

FIG. 31. JAVELIN
Strengthening

Mobility work is essential to the thrower and should be carried out daily. Whilst lack of strength may be a limiting factor for the thrower, lack of mobility is also a decided disadvantage for it prevents the athlete from working through the full range of movement.

Speed is obviously of importance to the thrower, for distance thrown is dependent upon speed of release of the implement. The ideal thrower is big, agile and sharp in his movements, not merely very big and sluggish. The thrower needs background running during the winter and spring and sprinting during the summer. He should be able to 'step in' and run a good leg on the club relay team.

Suggested schedules for a 17-year-old thrower
Winter and spring

> **Sunday**   20 plus throws working on one or two technical points. For the javelin thrower certainly these throws would be taken at less than full effort. For other throwers they would be taken at only slightly less than full effort – i.e. as fast as the athlete could manage and yet still think about the technical points. Javelin thrower to work from a short approach.
> 30 minutes fartlek.

(*Photos: Tissot van Patot*)

15. Bernd Kannenbert (Ger.) competing in the 20km. walk in Rome 1974 where he finished second in 1:29:38·2.

16. The Discus. Fainia Melr (USSR), the world record he shifts her body weight well the left foot before commen the drive across the circle

(Photo: Tony Duffy)

17. Klaus Wolfermann (Germany) Olympic Champion, Munich 1972 with 90.48m. Shows good form just prior to reaching the throwing position. Note the position of the hips and shoulders and the javelin extended well to the rear

(Photo: Tony Duffy)

Monday	Weight training, or Weight lifting.
Tuesday	Basket ball
Wednesday	Throwing practice, Weight training. Javelin thrower to use short approach and to throw a 4 pound weight.
Thursday	Gymnastics, 20 minute run.
Friday	———
Saturday	Major throwing session – throw until tired. Weight training.

Whilst it is preferable to throw on alternate days and not on consecutive days, it must be accepted that the problems of winter darkness may necessitate changes to the ideal schedule.

Mid-May

Sunday	20 plus throws, working on faults that were apparent during the previous day's competition. Javelin thrower to take easy throws with weight. Play at other events.
Monday	Weight training.
Tuesday	Main throwing session. 150 metre runs x 3 with a walk back recovery.
Wednesday	Weight training.
Thursday	Light throwing session. 60 metre sprints (from blocks) x 6 with adequate recovery.
Friday	Isometrics
Saturday	Competition.

Late June

Sunday	Rest or some form of exercise that provides a mental break from athletics, e.g. a day at the seaside.
Monday	Main throwing session, capitalising upon acquired skills and aiming to make only very minor technical changes. Weight training.
Tuesday	60 metre sprints (from blocks) x 6 with adequate recovery.

E

	Play at other events, e.g. jumping or hurdling.
Wednesday	Light throwing session.
	$\frac{1}{2}$ Weight training session.
Thursday	Easy running, including sharp bursts.
	Isometrics.
Friday	———
Saturday	Competition.

13 The Jumping Events and the Pole Vault

THE FUNDAMENTALS OF JUMPING ARE
  (a) A controlled approach run.
  (b) Control at the take-off.
  (c) Control in the air.
  (d) Control on landing.

(a) The approach run should be made at the greatest speed that the athlete can control and still jump effectively. Speed without control is of little value. The first problem of the jumper is to *jump*. His second problem is to be able to increase the speed at which he can jump effectively.

The jumper needs to think of his approach run as being the reproduction of a set pattern. One of the problems of the jumper is that he needs to eliminate from his performance any variables that are likely to be detrimental. He seeks to reproduce his ideal skill form for the event: he is striving after perfection. The jumper's aim in the approach run is to establish an accurate approach run pattern for every jump, and to do this at maximum speed. Once he is able to do this he can then concentrate on *jumping*.

Establishment of the Approach run – Long Jump, Triple Jump, Pole Vault.

(a) Before this can be done the athlete must have an adequate background of running (to include sprinting) in order to ensure an even stride length.

(b) *On the track* (100 metres straight)

From a standing start position, repetition 50 metre sprints should be carried out in order to establish a set pattern for the approach run. Once the length of the run has been decided a mark should be placed on the track to simulate the take off board and suitable check marks inserted. This approach should now be practised in training until it is consolidated. Only then should it be transferred to the runway. Now final adjustments can be made for the jump or vault.

(c) The athlete must be made to appreciate the importance of accurate measurement of approach runs, and should use a tape measure. In the jumps the measurement should be made from the front of the board. In the pole vault the measurement should be taken from the back of the box. The runway must be brushed so that the footmarks can be clearly distinguished.

(d) The athlete must be aware of the necessity of adjustment in the light of varying conditions. With a fast track and a following breeze the length of the approach run would be increased. In adverse conditions the length of the run would be decreased.

Some athletes like to hit a check mark after 3 strides (the strides that are likely to vary most. Other athletes, who have established consistency of stride length, use a rolling start, walking or jogging on to a predetermined start mark. Almost all athletes use a final check mark which is normally 8 strides from the board. The athlete may have to adjust slightly to hit this check, but he will then feel confident in his ability thereafter to hit the correct take-off spot. The usual total length of the approach run is 17, 19 or 21 strides.

Some athletes prefer their final check mark to be only 6 strides from the take-off. They are then close to top running speed, and can use this final check mark as a reminder of what is to follow – the preparation for the jump or vault. From this final check they think of driving into the jump or vault.

Establishment of the Approach run – High Jump

Probably the best plan for the novice jumper is to use a 7 stride approach run, possibly using a check mark 3 strides from the start of the run. Thus the high jumper who commences his run with the left foot will hit the check mark with the left foot and will jump off the left foot.

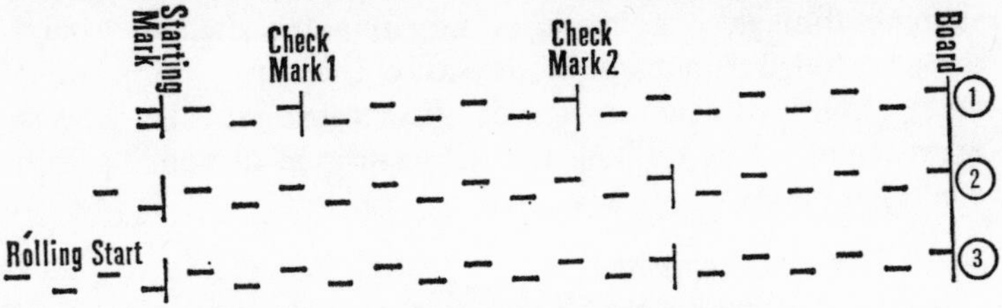

FIG. 32. POSITIONING OF CHECK MARKS

In all jumping events the importance of the correct approach run cannot be overstressed. An accurate approach run gives the athlete confidence and leaves him mentally rather more free to concentrate on the jump. The athlete who is not happy about his approach run is at a tremendous disadvantage. The coach should help the athlete to establish his approach run and must then be sure that the athlete knows how to make marginal adjustments in order to accommodate varying conditions.

Control at take-off. The movements leading up to take-off are important in as much as they enable the athlete to do the right things *at* take-off. In short, the athlete needs to be in a position to work at take-off – to drive maximally. One of the things that will help him to do this is to arrive at the correct take-off spot, at the correct speed and in the right position.

Control in the air. This is the ability to be in a position of balance in order to effect correct movements (required by the technique of the event) whilst in the air.

Control on landing. The landing is of obvious importance in terms of either distance gained or safety, or both of these factors.

Three of the above four factors necessitate a considerable amount of out-of-season jumping. Athletes need to keep in touch with the feel of jumping throughout much of the year.

We must guard against the attitude of some athletes who think that the sole factor of increased strength work during the winter will automatically lead to improved jumping performance during the summer. It *may* be that the dynamic factor of strength through jumping is as important as strength gained through weight training. In any case, jumping with control many times at slower speeds (increasing as the season approaches) seems to facilitate the acquisition of jumping with control at maximum speeds.

Safety factors in jumping
   (a) Firm, smooth runways that are free from ruts.
   (b) A take-off board that is 'flush' with the run up and not badly worn.
   (c) Protected heels. Sponge rubber heel pads were used in the past, but many athletes have now switched to plastic heel cups. These can be bought from the leading suppliers of sports equipment.
   (d) (Possibly) heel spikes rather than sprint spikes. This will depend upon the preferences of the athlete and the type of jumping surface.
   (e) A soft landing area that is free from hazards.
   (f) Roped runways to prevent other athletes walking across.
   (g) Strong legs and ankles!

LONG JUMP
General background

'A long jump can be thought of as a high jump at the end of a sprint.' Basically a simple event, the long jump involves an approach run of some 30 to 40 metres. The long jumper is a sprinter on the runway and aims to hit the take-off board at speed. However, the final 3 strides of the approach run show a slight variation from normal sprint technique as the long jumper drives less but puts himself in a better position for jumping *up*. He allows his centre of gravity to sink a little lower just before take-off in order that at take-off he can drive upwards, working the jumping leg through an optimum range.

There are two main techniques recommended for the action in the air:

1. The hitch kick, in which the jumper continues to run in the air, taking either $1\frac{1}{2}$ strides (a $1\frac{1}{2}$ hitch kick) or $2\frac{1}{2}$ strides. The jumper aims to keep the trunk upright and to work the knees round the hips, not the feet round the knees.
2. The 'hang', a less popular form of jumping and which is not as strongly recommended as the hitch kick. In the hang the athlete extends after take-off and holds this extended position until shortly before landing.

Qualities of the Long Jumper

Basic speed – the long jumper should be a good class sprinter, and must certainly be fast over a distance of 40 metres.

Spring – the long jumper should score highly (in excess of 60 cm.) on the vertical jump.

The ability to co-ordinate speed with spring.

Characteristics of a good Long Jump

1. A fast, smooth approach run to hit the take-off board.
2. A slight dip 1–2 strides before take-off.
3. A drive up from the board, giving the impression of height.
4. A well balanced action in the air, with the feet finally coming well forwards for the landing.

FIG. 33.   LONG JUMP
Drive *up at take-off*

Key features of long jumping
1. Drive in to take-off, hit the board at speed.
2. A bent knee position just before take-off.
3. An explosive jump upwards.
4. Trunk upright during the early phases of the jump.

Athlete should think about
1. Hitting the check mark and *driving* in aggressively.
2. (When within 3 strides of the board) *Jumping upwards.*
   Some athletes have been told to relax before take-off –
   but this is negative coaching. Relax they will ... but this
   relaxation will be accompanied by a considerable loss of
   speed. Better to think of driving in at speed, and then to
   think of height from the board. Probably the best thing
   to think of is of hips going high from the take-off. The
   athlete who thinks of head or chest height may throw
   his head back and get false impression of height.
3. (If performing the $1\frac{1}{2}$ hitch kick): Drive up powerfully
   from take-off, particularly with the 'spare' knee. Hold
   this position fractionally and *then* go into the hitch kick,
   thinking about working the legs round the hips and of a
   long sweep back of the leading (non-jumping) leg.

Coaching positions
1. On rare occasions the coach will stand with the athlete
   running towards him, and will check for swerve on the
   runway or for an off-line take-off.
2. The main coaching position is some 20 metres back and
   at right angles to the runway. From here the coach will
   watch for the following faults.

Major fault 1:
Inability to hit take-off board, *or* having to chop stride in order
to hit board.
  Correction:
  See section on
  'Establishment of the approach run.'

Major fault 2:
Slowing in the approach run.

Correction:

(a) Ensure that approach run is correct.

(b) Ensure that jumping leg is strong enough to work at speed.

(c) Think of accelerating in from the check mark. Note that this may mean that both approach run and check mark need to be brought a little closer to the board, for the acceleration may cause staccato striding.

Major fault 3:

No height from the board – athlete simply sprinting and then lifting the feet from under himself rather than jumping.

Correction:

(a) Lots of jumping and bounding out-of-season.

(b) Adequate leg strength.

(c) Jumping for height from a short run. As the season approaches the length and speed of this run must be increased and the athlete must still jump high.

(d) Drive up with spare knee.

(e) Accentuate arm drive at take-off.

Major fault 4:

Athlete unbalanced in the air.

Correction:

(a) More out-of-season jumping.

(b) Aim to extend at take-off and to keep the body upright during the early part of the jump.

Major fault 5:

Completing the $1\frac{1}{2}$ hitch kick too soon and 'collapsing' on landing.

Correction:

(a) Delay the hitch kick action off the board. Hold the spare knee high briefly (before going into the hitch kick).

or

(b) (If the distance covered is in excess of 7 metres) consider the use of a $2\frac{1}{2}$ hitch kick.

Major fault 6:

In the hang technique, the trunk coming forwards to the legs, resulting in a poor landing position.

Correction:

(a) Emphasise a powerful take-off and swing back of the lead leg.

(b) Bring the legs through bent and then straighten them late for landing.

TRIPLE JUMP

General principles

Whilst the term 'hop, step and jump' is an adequate description of the event for the teaching of schoolboys, the term 'triple jump' is more appropriate in coaching. In effect there *are* 3 jumps, and the athlete strives for distance on each phases. Not maximum distance on each phase, but that combination of distances that will lead to maximum total distance. The athlete aims for *optimum* distance on the first two phases – i.e. the greatest distance that he can achieve and still be in a position to work effectively for the next phase. He aims for maximum distance on the final jump.

Triple jumpers generally hop from their stronger leg – i.e. they work from the stronger leg twice and the weaker leg once. The technique of the event may be thought of in one of three ways:

1. As a rhythm which sounds to be almost evenly spaced: thump ... thump ... thump
2. As an increase in height on each phase.
3. As a spacing ratio for each of the 3 phases, with the ratio being

Hop		Step		Jump
4	:	3	:	4

This spacing ratio represents an approximate guide for the triple jumper, and it must be noted that there are two major divisions of triple jump technique:

(a) The 'Flat' or 'Polish' technique, in which the ratio is approximately:

Hop	Step	Jump
35%	30%	35%

(b) The Russian technique, in which the ratio is approximately

Hop	Step	Jump
38%	30%	32%

The main difference between the two techniques is that the Polish technique involves a slightly lower hop. This means that slightly less distance is covered during the first phase, but that the athlete is better able to conserve speed for the remaining phases. The 'sprinter' type of triple jumper tends towards the 'Polish' method whilst the 'bounding' athlete (strong legs, light body) tends towards the 'Russian' method. In working with the club athlete the coach will probably tend towards the 'Polish ' method, but will obviously be influenced by the physique of the athlete.

Qualtities of the the Triple Jumper

The triple jumper needs:
(a) The basic speed of the sprinter. Like the long jumper, the triple jumper should aim to hold his place on a club or school relay team.
(b) To have strong legs. The triple jumper is usually light in the body and 'bouncy', and his legs are capable of 'working' even after the tremendous stress of landing.

Characteristics of a good Triple Jump

(a) A fast, accurate approach with the athlete increasing leg cadence over the final 6 strides.
(b) Athlete to *run* off the board rather than bound.
(c) *Relatively* little loss of forward speed on each landing. (In effect there is probably a loss of approximately 1–2 metres per second of forward speed at each contact).
(d) Active landings – the athlete appears to be working at each phase of the event. The emphasis here should be on the foot coming down and back for each landing, and the landing to be a 'flat foot' landing.
(e) In a good triple jump the coach gets the impression of controlled power, with one phase of the event flowing into the next.

FIG. 34.   TRIPLE JUMP

(a) *Accelerate into the take-off and drive forwards rather than upwards.* (b) *Trunk upright and hold the knee high.* (c) *Landings to be flat-footed and active.* (d) *Drive into the step.* (e) *Trunk upright and a wide split between the thighs.* (f) *The leading foot moves backwards just prior to landing.* (g) *Maximum effort and good height into the jump*

Athlete to think about

(a) Accelerating to the board, and then maintaining speed throughout the jump. (Although this is not possible, it is nevertheless a good thought for the athlete.)

(b) Hop to be low and fast.

(c) Of aiming for a wide split between the thighs at each take-off, with the thigh of the non-take-off leg held high.

(d) Working at each phase, bringing the foot down and back for each landing. The reasonably skilled athlete should aim to use the arms vigorously.

(e) Keeping the trunk upright in the air.

Coaching position

Approximately 20 metres back from the runway, usually opposite the point of landing for the hop.

Major fault 1:

Inability to hit take-off board, *or* having to chop or stretch stride in order to hit board.

Correction:

See section on

'Establishment of the Approach run.'

Major fault 2:

Slowing in the approach run.

Correction:

(a) Ensure that the approach run is correct.

(b) Think of accelerating in from the check mark.

Major fault 3:

A 'dead' take-off from the board.

Correction:

(a) Think of accelerating in from the check mark.

(b) Think of an aggressive take off and of running forward powerfully from the board at take-off.

(c) Think of reaching forwards and upwards with the spare knee.

Major fault 4:

Hop too high, with the result that the leg almost buckles on landing.

Correction:

(a) Think of forward movement from the take-off board rather than upward movement.

(b) Ensure an adequacy of leg strength.

Major fault 5:

A short step.

This is the most common fault in triple jumping.

Correction:

(a) This *may* be the result of the previous fault. Initially the coach would suggest corrections as for fault (4).

(b) The fault may have been caused simply by the athlete trying to go too far on the hop. The athlete must accept a slight loss of distance on the hop in order to be in a position to go for greater distance on the step.

(c) Maintain the 'trunk upright' position in the hop. If the athlete is off balance and leaning too far forwards as he lands from the hop, then the step can only be a recovery.

(d) Ensure that on landing from the hop the athlete is not reaching forwards with the heel of the landing foot. The athlete must think of flat-footed, active landings.

(e) Ensure that the athlete in 'working' into the step: if necessary, think of drive with the arms and the spare knees.

Major fault 6:

Undue loss of speed at each phase.

Correction:

(a) Ensure that the athlete is not going too high. Height is only good if the athlete is strong enough to cope with the landing after going high.

(b) Think of flat-footed landings with the foot moving back.

Major fault 6a:

Jarred landings.

Correction:

Point 6 (b) above.

Major fault 7:

A poor jump.

   Correction:

   (a) This may possibly be caused by over-reaching on the step, in which case the correction in point 6 (b) above.

   (b) Think of driving back with the jumping leg.

   (c) Long jump practice from the 'wrong' leg.

Form in the jump will depend upon the distance being covered. If the athlete has lost much of his forward speed at the end of the step, then he will probably use the 'Sail' technique, which is really no technique at all – he merely tries to keep the feet forward and the trunk reasonably upright. With a rather better jump, then he will probably use the 'Hang' technique.

HIGH JUMP

General principles

   The Fosbury technique has been in operation for over a decade, ever since Dick Fosbury won a Gold Medal with his innovation in style in the Mexico Olympic Games, 1964. Undoubtedly this technique has given thousands of young high jumpers the opportunity and incentive to become champions. The technically excellent and uninhibited take-off achieved by jumpers using this method gives it an immediate advantage over the more complicated Straddle technique. However, even after this period of time the Straddle is still 'holding its own' in international class high jumping. This is undoubtedly because when it has been well taught, and therefore, well executed it still has certain mechanical advantages over the Fosbury style of jumping. This section, will therefore, deal first with the Straddle and then with the Fosbury method of take-off and bar clearance.

   The modern straddle jumper adds *swing* to *spring*. To the spring of the jumping leg he adds the swing of the free leg and of both arms. The basic principle is that the athlete must strive to evoke the greatest possible force against the ground in order to project his centre of gravity as high as possible. The swing of the arms and of the free leg will add to 'lift' at take-off. The high jumper also aims to work through the greatest possible range at take off. Hence the modern jumper comes in to take off a little lower than his counterpart of some 10 years ago. Just prior to take off there is a greater bend at the knee of the jumping leg and the athlete then works through a greater range as he drives upwards.

The modern straddle jumper also works at a greater speed than his counterpart of 10 years ago. By performing the movements at a greater speed, and by increasing the acceleration of the free leg swing, the athlete is able to evoke an even greater force at take-off. As coaches we need to note that in addition to the switch to the straddle technique, there has also been considerable modification within the technique. Greater speed and length of the approach run have also necessitated a narrowing of the angle of the approach run. With some athletes the angle of the approach run is as little as 25 degrees to the bar.

Qualities of the High Jumper
  (a) Natural spring.
  (b) A feeling for body orientation.

Characteristics of a good High Jump technique
  (a) A balanced approach run, gathering to an aggressive take off.
  (b) A low position during the final two strides (but not *too* low, for it must be a position from which the jumper is

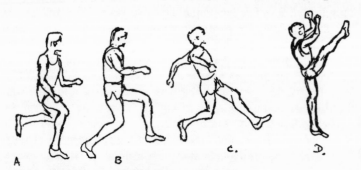

FIG. 35.   HIGH JUMP
(a, b) Come in low. (c) Long last stride and attack the take-off. (d) Free leg swing

still able to drive up effectively – and strength is required for this).

(c) A long last stride.

(d) A free leg swing, preferably straight when in the horizontal position and accelerating maximally when horizontal.

(e) Lift from the arms.

Athlete to think about

(a) Coming in low.

(b) Long last stride and attack the take-off. (The great high jumpers think about take off rather than clearance).

(c) Exploding upwards!

Coaching emphasis

The basis of the bar clearance is quickly learnt, providing that a safe built-up landing area is available. Indeed, one of the problems of the coach lies in dealing with youngsters whose bar clearance is immaculate, but who do not jump very high!

FIG. 36. STRADDLE CLEARANCE

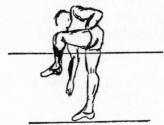

FIG. 37. STRADDLE CLEARANCE PRACTICE
*Outwardly rotate the rear knee and fall over
onto the back*

The emphasis in coaching should be upon *take-off*. As a prerequisite to this good take-off, the athlete needs to arrive on the correct take-off spot, well balanced and at a speed that he is able to control. During the early sessions of straddle jumping it might be wise to limit the athlete to an approach run of 5 strides. However, as the athlete increases his strength and his ability to cope with the take-off technique he will need to lengthen his approach run and decrease the angle of approach.

Coaching positions
1. *At a right angle to the take-off* check
   1. The smoothness of the approach run.
   2. 'Attack' at take-off.
   3. Long last stride.
   4. Free leg swing (and, with a competent performer, the swing of the arms).
2. *In line with the bar check*
   1. Position of the athlete's high point relative to the bar.
   2. The position of the athlete over the bar.
   3. *With the athlete running towards the coach*
      Check to ensure that the athlete is jumping *up* and that he is not leaning too much towards the bar at take-off.

Major fault 1:
A pattering approach run.
   Correction:
   Measured approach run, possibly with a check mark.

Major fault 2:
Too much forward travel at take-off, causing too much length in the jump and not enough height.
   Correction:
   (a) Long last stride.
   (b) Running in low rather than settling at the take-off spot.
   (c) An earlier drive up from the take-off leg.

Major fault 3:
Turning too early over the bar and failing to get height in the jump.

Correction:
(a) Concentrate on jumping up, paying for more attention to this than to bar clearance.
(b) Elevate inside shoulder.

Major fault 4:
Lack of free leg swing.

Correction:
It is difficult to correct this fault. Initially the coach needs to be sure that the athlete has enough hip mobility to go for free leg swing: then he needs to work for free leg swing
(a) without the bar – sometimes running forwards and jumping (without the turn) to kick high;
(b) Elevate inside shoulder.
concentrating on free leg swing and feeling that he is being lifted from the ground by the free leg.
(c) Increase height of bar and continue to work for free leg swing.
(d) Think of swinging arms as well.

Major fault 5:
Taking bar off with foot of free leg on the way up.

Correction:
Aim the free leg swing much higher than the bar and delay the turn.

Major fault 6:
Taking the bar off with the thigh of the rear (jumping) leg.

Correction:
When the leg bends after take-off, allow it to stay bent and then outwardly rotate the leg away from the bar.
This can be practised as a ground exercise.

Major fault 7:
Taking the bar off with the chest.

Correction:
This fault is usually caused by the athlete throwing the rear leg and the head back in an attempt to clear the bar. By virtue of action and reaction, this forces the chest down.
Correction (6) above.

FOSBURY TECHNIQUE

With the introduction of foam rubber landing areas which are built up well above ground level, wide enough and deep enough to absorb with safety any kind of landing, the Fosbury Flop has come into its own at all levels of high jumping.

The style has the advantage of a simple 'outside foot' take-off, which, off a curved approach run, leads to a direct upward thrust with the body weight directly over the jumping leg. This means that the most important part of the jump is correctly performed from the beginning without any complicated technique having to be mastered, as in the straddle jump.

However, it must be remembered that this is a thoroughly dangerous style unless a more than adequate landing area is provided. Also boys and girls learning this method should be supervised by a teacher, at least until they are performing competently.

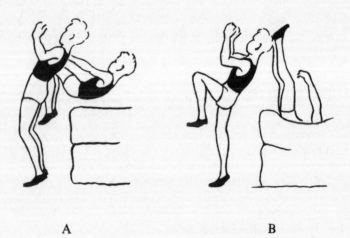

A   B

C   D

FIG. 38.   THE FOSBURY TECHNIQUE

Teaching stages

1. Find out which foot the athletes wish to jump off by asking them to perform a simple scissor jump off a short approach run. The stronger jumping leg will be established during the first lesson.

2. Without a crossbar, face away from the foam rubber pit, jump off both feet and back drop into the landing area. Fig. 38 (a).

3. Repeat this practice but take off from the jumping leg alone. Fig. 38 (b).

4. The class should now be divided, left-footed jumpers going to the right side of the pit and right-footed jumpers to the left. As many pits as are available should be used and the groups be made as small as possible. Taking the right footed athlete as an example, the jumpers should approach from the left hand side off a three stride run and jump, turning on the back as before and dropping into the pit. Fig. 38 (c-d).

5. The bar should now be inserted at a low height and the children asked to perform off this short run. The bar can be raised gradually and the run slightly increased until it

F

is time to teach a correct approach run.

6. Assuming the take-off point to be a metre in from the upright and approximately the same distance out from the bar, work back on a full half curve for 9 strides. The athletes should practise this approach first of all slowly and then gradually at an increased tempo until they are confident about reaching the take-off spot on every occasion.

7. The bar is now once more inserted and the height increased little by little. The curving approach will mean the children are leaning away from the bar when they plant the take-off foot.

The teacher should be careful to emphasise that the take-off is a long upward drive and not just a hurried twist off the ground. The jumpers should be encouraged to stress the following points:—

1. Lean away from the bar as the foot is planted for take-off.

2. Make themselves as tall as possible or imagine they are heading a football directly above their heads as they leave the ground.

3. Swing up the inside knee (free leg) because this helps with lift and rotation to cross the bar on the back.

4. As they lift towards the bar, turn the inside shoulder (shoulder nearest to the bar) back towards the run-up. This will help with the turn and lay-out.

5. As the child crosses the bar, the emphasis should be on a big arch of the body with the hips up. When the hips are over, the knees bend and the head begins to lift.

6. After the body has crossed the lath, the legs are straightened and the body jack-knifed with the head and shoulders coming up to help clear the legs from the bar.

7. Relax for the landing on the back.

POLE VAULT

Whilst this event is a pole *vault* and not a pole *jump* it is best considered with the jumping events. Like the long jumper and triple jumper, the pole vaulter needs speed on the runway, and like other jumpers he needs an aggressive take-off.

General principles

The height cleared in the vault depends upon two factors:

1. How high the vaulter is able to hold the pole and bring it to a vertical position – and this in turn depends upon
   (a) The flexibility of the pole.
   (b) The approach speed co-ordinating with
   (c) spring from the correct take-off spot.
   (d) The ability to keep the body weight low relative to the grip during the initial stages of the vault.
   (e) Strength.
2. How high the athlete is able to push himself over his hands in order to clear the bar. This depends upon
   (a) Physical skill.
   (b) Strength, and the ability to use this strength at speed.

Qualities of the Pole Vaulter

1. Basic speed
2. Strength.
3. Body orientation – the ability to know where he is during the vault.
4. Gymnastic ability.
5. Courage.

Key features of a good performance using a metal pole.

1. A balanced approach run at the maximum controlled speed.
2. A smooth handshift (bottom hand going up to top hand) and early planting of the pole.
3. An aggressive take-off, driving upwards.
4. The 'hang' behind the pole in the early stages of the vault.
5. Hips up, knees up and body going close to the vertical.
6. A vigorous pull to zip off the top of the pole, still moving upwards.

Athlete should think about

1. Accelerating into the take-off.
2. An early plant.

FIG. 39.   POLE VAULT
(a) Attack the take-off. (b) Rock back, hold the body away from the pole. (c) Stay back! (d) The turn comes late and fast with the hips high, and there is a 1–2 release of the hands

3. Look forward and w-a-i-t.
4. Exploding into . . . 'Knees up, hips up and PULL.'

Coaching the pole vault
   Faults evident at one stage of an event can often be traced

back to faults earlier in the event. In the pole vault, faults seen in the air can often be traced back to faults at take-off. Consistency at take-off is of paramount importance, and early coaching (which follows the success of early *teaching*) should be mainly directed at securing an efficient take-off. For a novice pole vaulter the length of the approach run is unlikely to be in excess of 20 metres. Considerable attention should be given to a smooth take-off, with the take-off foot (toe) being under the top hand at the take-off. When this has been achieved it is important for the athlete to pause (look forward and extend the body) immediately after take-off rather than letting the hips drift forward. As in many other activities, the head is the guide.

Only when the above skills have been mastered is the athlete able to move on to skilful bar clearance work. Before this stage has been reached, of course, the athlete will be doing some work over a bar, because this is the essence of the fun of pole vaulting. However the coach will constantly need to bring the athlete back to the fundamentals of 'take-off' and 'hang' as prerequisites to excellent clearance.

Coaching positions
1. Almost all coaching will be done from about 20 metres back from the runway, at right angles to the take-off spot. The major faults listed below can best be seen from this position.
2. Occasionally the coach may need to stand behind the athlete to ensure that he is taking off in line with the line of run. If his take-off is 'off-line', then the correction is for him to think of an early plant.

(Metal pole)
Major fault 1:
Inability to hit the correct take-off spot.

   Correction:
   (a) See 'Establishment of the Approach Run'.
   (b) When the take-off is consistently too close, think of an early plant.
Major fault 2:
Inability to 'hang – swinging past the pole too soon.

Correction:
(a) Check the take-off.
If this is correct, *then*
(b) Look forward immediately after take-off instead of looking at the bar.

Major fault 3:
Hips away from the pole at the top of the vault.
Correction:
(a) Improve 'hang' as indicated above.
(b) Think of the hips eventually going *up* rather than *across* the bar.

Major fault 4:
Swinging round the pole at the top of the vault.
Correction:
Check the take-off – it is probably 'off-line'. Plant early.

Major fault 5:
Getting up in the vault and then dropping down on to the bar.
Correction:
(a) Lower the grip on the pole, *or*
(b) hang longer.
Note that the correct position for the stands is usually 30 cm. to 60 cm. back from the line of the vertical pole.

Major fault 6:
Taking the bar off with the chest.
Correction:
(a) Ensure that the stands are in the correct position.
(b) Raise the grip.

Major fault 7:
Top grip slipping down the pole.
Correction:
(a) This is usually the result of a take-off that is too close to the box. Work for an early plant.
(b) In rainy conditions the athlete may have difficulty in gripping the pole. He should

1. Keep the pole grip dry between vaults.
2. Smear the top grip with *venice turpentine* – obtainable from some chemists.

Key features of a good performance using a fibre glass pole
1. A balanced approach run at maximum controlled speed, with the athlete giving the impression that he is accelerating into the take-off.
2. A partial handshift only (30 cm. apart) and an early plant with the athlete driving *forwards* at take-off.
3. A pole bend, with the athlete holding himself away from the pole with a flexed lower arm.
4. A rock back into the 'kip' position, with the hips being held high.
5. A late turn, twisting along the long axis of the body.

Athlete should think about
1. Accelerating in and planting early.
2. Driving forwards at take-off.
3. Holding the body away from the pole.
4. Rocking back and staying back.

(Fibre glass pole)
Major fault 1:
Retaining metal pole technique.

Correction:
(a) This is partly psychological – the vaulter must accept retrogression before progression.
(b) Concentrate on bend, driving the lower arm forward at take-off.

Major fault 2:
Little bend.
Correction:
(a) Ensure that the pole is not too stiff for the vaulter. A vaulter weighing, say, 155 lbs would probably start fibre glass vaulting on a pole designed for a man weighing up to 150 lbs.

(b) Use a wider grasp on the pole, holding as far as 70 cm. between the hands. As the ability to bend the pole is acquired, then work for bend from a partial handshift.

Major fault 3:
Slipping the top grip.

Correction:
(a) Use *venice turpentine.*
(b) Check the take-off spot – it may be too close.
(c) Think of an early plant.

Major fault 4:
Drifting way from the pole at the top.

Correction:
(a) During the early stages of the vault think of maintaining the position away from the pole and keeping the bend.
(b) Think of rocking back even further, and do not anticipate the clearance.

Major fault 5:
Vault 'dying' before the bar is reached.

Correction:
(a) Ensure that the grip is not *too* high.
(b) Work on points 4a and 4b.
(c) More aggressive take-off.

TRAINING FOR THE JUMPS AND FOR THE POLE VAULT

General
Running training should be carried on throughout the year. The athlete should work on fartlek and repetition uphill work during the winter, giving way to interval work during the spring. During the summer there will still be a little interval work, but most of the running training will be either easy jogging and striding on grass or else very fast sprint work on the track. *Jumping or vaulting* will normally be included twice a week

throughout winter, spring and summer. Skill in the jumping events is not easy to acquire and only the very skilful athlete can afford a lay-off from winter skill training – and even this may not be advisable. Much jumping during the winter will lay a firm foundation for skilful performances during the summer and will aid the development of jumping strength. The jumper will often work upon aspects of technique from a short approach run – perhaps 5 strides in the high jump and 9–11 strides in the other jumping events.

Strength training is carried on almost throughout the year, with a considerable amount of work during the winter and spring, tapering to a minimum quantity during the peak season. All-round strength is required by the jumper, and to this all-round training he might add exercises specific to his event. Thus the pole vaulter would add rope climb and chins to his weight training schedule whilst the triple jumper would add step-ups with a weight across his shoulders.

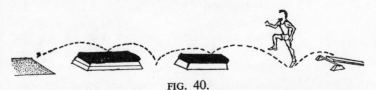

FIG. 40.

INDOOR STRENGTH-SKILL TRAINING FOR THE TRIPLE JUMP

Strength training for the jumper, however, means much more than weight training. Constant repetition of a maximum effort take-off is useful to both high jumper and long jumper. Repetition hopping, repetition hop-hop-step, hopping uphill, hopping and bounding from box tops are all strength activities of value to the triple jumper. Apparatus gymnastics, the evelopment of strength in swinging movements is of utmost importance to the pole vaulter. Certainly the jumper must think in terms of the development of strength in activities similar to his event, in addition to his weight training.

Mobility work should be carried out at the beginning of each training session.

Winter competition can provide a useful measure of progress and an incentive. Jumpers and vaulters, together with sprinters, hurdlers and shot putters, can take advantage of indoor com-

petition. Training should not be biased towards winter competition unless the athlete has a chance of major honours (and
is unlikely to achieve those honours during the outdoor season),
but should be taken as part of the normal training plan.

The coach should also arrange competitions in various
ancillary aspects of the event. He can also plan for a number
of interesting competitions based on the 'Jumping Decathlon
Tables' listed in the appendix.

Suggested schedules for a 17-year-old Jumper or Vaulter
Winter – Spring

Sunday	Fartlek, supplementary leg strengthening work.
Monday	Weight training.
Tuesday	Basketball or activity of a similar nature – e.g. a 'non-contact' sport which demands quick movements.
Wednesday	Jumping or vaulting for form, often from a short approach run. Many jumps. Fartlek (in winter) or Interval training (in spring), to include supplementary leg strengthening work.
Thursday	Gymnastics, Vaulter to include apparatus work. Weight training.
Friday	———
Saturday	Main jumping or vaulting session, varied with occasional competition days. Vaulter to add upper body strengthening work – e.g. work on parallel or horizontal bars, on rings or on pommel horse: or rope climb or chins.

Mid-May

Sunday	Selected aspects of technique work, (possibly from a short approach). Interval running – 150 metres fast stride x 5 with 4 minute recovery.
Monday	Weight training (*and* gymnastics for the pole vaulter).
Tuesday	20 minutes easy running on grass.
Wednesday	Technique work from full approach – perhaps

efforts at slightly less than maximum effort, but aiming for technical excellence.

Supplementary strength training.

Thursday   50 metres sprints from blocks x 6 (adequate recovery): hurdles.

½ Weight training session.

Friday   ———

Saturday   Competition.

Late June – early July

Sunday   Rest *or* complete change – possibly day at seaside or walk in hills.

Monday   Technique work – main training day – some work from a full approach, and then, when tiring, possibly some work from a short approach on specific points.

Supplementary strength training.

Tuesday   Weight training. *Add* gymnastics for the pole vaulter.

20 minutes easy run on grass.

Wednesday   50 metres sprints from blocks x 6 with adequate recovery.

Technique work – brief session.

Supplementary strength training.

Thursday   20 minutes easy running on grass.

Friday   ———

Saturday   Competition.

14 The Decathlon

General background
The 10 events of the Decathlon are contested in this order:

First day	100 metre run
	Long Jump
	Shot Put
	High Jump
	400 metre run.
Second day	110 metres High hurdles
	Discus Throw
	Pole Vault
	Javelin Throw
	1500 metre run.

Performances in each event receive points on the basis of the level of performance. Scoring is from the I.A.A.F. Scoring Tables. Competitors must participate in each of the 10 events. Three trials only are allowed in the Long Jump, Shot Put, Discus Throw and Javelin Throw.

Qualities of the 'Decathlete'
Basically the decathlete is big, fast and strong. He is not an athlete who has failed to make the grade in other events – he is an athlete who rates highly in his specialist events and who also thinks of himself as being primarily interested in the Decathlon. He is almost certainly a competent high hurdler – usually a brawny one. He is also a 'skill-hungry athlete' who

18. *Above left:* Mike Bull (Queen's University and Gt Britain) driving fowards at the take-off in the Pole Vault

19. *Above right:* Mike Bull again. Stay on the back and turn late

20. The Long Jump. Randy Williams (USA) Olympic Champion, Munich 1972, keeping the trunk upright

(Photo: Tony Duffy)

21. Tests and Measurements. Banked boards for the shuttle run

22. Tests and Measurements. The back and leg dynamometer: for back strength

likes playing at the skills of various events. He is also of equable temperament, accustomed to the length competition of the Decathlon, and to the constant need for relaxation between events and the further warm-ups as he moves to the next event.

Training for the Decathlon

The general principles of training for the various events have already been outlined, and the points related to skill, strength and speed training are as applicable to the decathlete as they are to any other athlete. Most of the decathlete's stamina training is incidental to his training, for as he works on a number of events he inevitably builds up some stamina, particularly from his fartlek and interval running. He does not train specifically for the 1,500 metres, because the time that he would spend improving in this event would be more wisely spent on speed or skill work for other events. He would, however, find that much of his training for the hurdles, for the jumps and for the throws bears a close resemblance to the training followed by a specialist in those events. The decathlete must try to resolve the problem of working for relative efficiency in 10 events, and must bear in mind that the demands of one event may conflict slightly with the demands of another event. He must apportion his time and efforts in order to gain the greatest number of points possible in the Decathlon, rather than concentrating on one or two events.

Decathlon training – general points

1. Athlete to work for speed, for this factor underlies almost all of the decathlon events.
2. Athlete to work for strength, and his strength training must lead to the power of the sprinter, jumper or thrower.
3. Athlete to work for skilled performance in the technical events, and must bear in mind that it is as important to improve his strengths as it is to eliminate his weaknesses. Skill training presents the greatest problem for the athlete, since it is difficult to balance out the demands of different events. It is not easy for the coach to suggest training schedules that are satisfying in the all-round sense. What the decathlete must do is accept that he may need to work

on a limited range of events in order to acquire basic skills. When his skill level in an event is good, then the 'little and often' principle will suffice to maintain skill, whilst he gives the main focus of his attention to the acquisition of new skills.

Winter and early spring training is for work on basic skills, working on two or perhaps 3 events for perhaps 3 months – long enough to show progress – before switching to another two events. It may be that one event is carried through the whole of the out-of-season period. The choice of events to work on will obviously depend upon the technical strengths and weaknesses of the individual athlete. Hence in the reasonable weather of autumn and early winter the athlete might work to improve, say, High Hurdles, Pole Vault and Discus. In the poorer weather of January and February he might concentrate upon a block of work based upon technique work for the Shot Put and Long Jump (from a short approach), for both of these events can be practised in weather that would be impossible for pole vaulting. During this same late winter and early spring period the athlete would consolidate his strength training and do some fartlek work or interval training.

Winter and early spring training, therefore, is for:

1. Running
2. Strength training
3. Technique training, working on a 'block' of dissimilar events.

During the late spring period the athlete should sharpen up on his interval running, reduce the quantity of strength training and re-establish contact with the other technical events.

Late spring is for:

1. Running, but with a greater emphasis on speed-stamina repetition work.
2. Strength training, but with a greater element of power.
3. A widening range of skill work. During this period, and during the summer, the athlete should be 'in contact' with all the technical events. He should aim to practise each technical event at least once a fortnight.

Summer is for:
1. Sprint training.
2. Less strength training – just enough to 'keep in touch' with the weights. During the summer the athlete works less often with weights, reducing to once a week. In this session he maintains the poundages of spring, but reduces both sets and repetitions.
3. A full range of skill work.
4. Competition. The decathlon is a demanding event and it would be unwise to compete too frequently. During the season it would seem reasonable to compete, perhaps, at intervals of 3 weeks. When no decathlon competition is available then the athlete should compete in selected events at other meetings. He should compete in 3 or 4 events, and should certainly include those events in which competition is important and difficult to obtain, such as the hurdles.

SUGGESTED TRAINING SCHEDULE FOR A 20-YEAR-OLD ATHLETE FOR DECATHLON

	Winter	*Spring*	*Summer*
Sunday	Skill training (2 events)	Skill training (2 events)	Easy run away from track – seaside or country.
Monday	Fartlek Weight training, Basketball.	Interval running Weight training, Basketball.	½ Weight training session, Skill practice (2 or 3 events).
Tuesday	Resistance running.	Resistance running.	Sprints or hurdles: one throwing event.
Wednesday	Skill training (2 events)	Skill training (2 events)	———
Thursday	———	———	Skill practice (2 events): very fast, easy strides.
Friday	Weight training, Gymnastics.	Weight training, Gymnastics.	———
Saturday	Skill training (2 events)	Skill training (2 events)	Competition in selected events.

Skill training may involve the athlete working on the same event on more than one day of the week. During the winter schedule, for example, the athlete will be practising 3 events.

The coach needs to ensure that the athlete does not visit the track too often. Many athletes in this event feel that they should be at the track daily. This would be unwise because it might easily lead to staleness. The coach should plan for a maximum of 4 track sessions a week, and should also plan for some relaxed running away from the track.

15 Tests and Measurements in Athletic Training

We live in a world of measurement, for measurement enables us to compare, and helps us to evaluate performances and abilities. To the athlete the most important yardstick is the measure of performance in his selected event. Other forms of testing and measurement may be prescribed by the coach for a variety of reasons, but they must be limited in number. There have been cases of athletes attending courses and being tested to such an extent that they were not fully able to partake in the course of training! The criterion of the coach must be:

'Can this testing teach us something that will ultimately help the athlete's performance?'

If the answer to the above question is 'Yes', then the coach should plan to do some testing, selecting his tests with care and testing but rarely. Above all he must remember that much of the athlete's training is a naïve form of testing, and that performance in the selected event is far more important than other tests.

There are two forms of testing and measurement in training:
1. Testing and Measurement as a Science
When the coach uses tests and measurements in the manner in which testing would be carried out by a scientist, then he must ensure that the tests satisfy the following requirements:

(a) *Validity* – the test must measure what it claims to measure.
(b) *Reliability* – the consistency of a measure. If the coach

165

measures a group of athletes on a particular test and then measures them a week later on the same test (without intervening practice by the athlete), then he should expect much the same results.

(c) *Objectivity* – that two coaches would test in the same way and get the same results on the administration of a particular test.

(d) *Simplicity* – the test should be easy to administer and should be cheap, for the coach cannot afford a considerable amount of time for his testing, neither can be afford considerable expense for equipment.

It is also wise to use a test for which 'norms' are available. This means that a vast number of people have been tested on the test, and that on the basis of this previous testing a scale has been drawn up to indicate how good performances are, ranging from 'Excellent' down to 'Very Poor'. The coach must be rather wary about the interpretation of 'norms', bearing in mind that 'norms' have usually been calculated from almost the full range of possible performance in an activity, whereas the athletes represent a special group at the top end of the range. Nevertheless the coach can gain some value from the 'norms', comparing the athlete with the known performances of other athletes and with his own performance (say) two months hence.

Athletes must be warmed up for the tests in the same way each time, the value of the tests should be explained to the athlete and the results interpreted to the athletes.

There are a multitude of tests that can be used. The coach must decide upon the quality that he wishes to measure and then upon the most suiable test for the measurement of that quality. There would be relatively little point, for instance, in measuring the endurance of a shot putter, for we are more interested in his strength and power.

Some of the tests in common usage are:

Strength

Grip strength as shown on a grip dynamometer.

Back lift ⎫
Left lift ⎭ as shown on a 'Back and leg' dynamometer.

Muscular endurance

Chins (i.e. the maximum number of chins that an athlete can perform for the 'hanging overgrasp' position)
(Chins are also known as 'pull-ups')

Dips (the maximum number of dips that an athlete can perform between parallel bars)

Power

Vertical Jump (the height that an athlete can jump from both feet *above* his normal reach height)

Standing long jump

FIG. 41.   VERTICAL JUMP

General endurance (a cardio vascular test)

Harvard Step Test.

Motor Fitness test (A test of good condition for speed and power events)

Phillips JCR test.

In all testing the coach should carefully follow the instructions of the test. Both coach and athlete should keep a record of the results of the test.

Details of the above tests and of many other tests are given in: Campbell W. R. and Tucker N. R., *An Introduction to Tests and Measurements in Physical Education.*

2. *Testing and Measurement as an Art*

There are times when the coach functions as a scientist, and there are other times when his task is that of a lay psychologist. At times coaching becomes an art. In the field of tests and measurements the coach may be justified in taking the tests out of their scientific context and using tests of his own design if he feels that this will benefit the athlete. These tests will often take the form of a training trial. The coach might time the athlete over a woodland circuit, and then set him a target for a run a month hence. The coach might measure the distance that a triple jumper can cover in 5 hops. Or he might measure the time that it takes a hurdler to get to the 'touch-down' after the third hurdle. Tests of this type can rarely be described as 'scientific': yet they are often of value. When the coach uses this approach to his testing, he is using tests as an incentive. The tests should be:

(a) Interesting.
(b) Related to the event – and the athlete must be able to see this relationship.
(c) Related to the individual
  – to his previous work
  – to his future targets
  – and perhaps to the known performances of other athletes.

The Values of Tests and Measurements in a training programme are:

1. To help the athlete to overcome the problem of winter training for a short summer season – to provide variety and maintain interest – and to acknowledge that many athletes thrive both emotionally and socially on

competition.

2. To get a group or team together for purposeful work which may be rather different from the normal plan of training. The coach will occasionally measure performance in 'odd' events such as

   50 metres timed run pulling a garden roller.
   Weight lifted in a 'Power' clean.

3. To motivate, possibly by drawing comparisons.

4. To diagnose physical weaknesses and then to suggest improvements in the training programme. To measure the improvements that the changed training programme has brought about.

5. As a training discipline. Measurement of performance in a demanding test is occasionally a useful way of obtaining maximum training effort from the athlete.

6. To give confidence to the athlete. If records have been kept and it is obvious that progress has been maintained, then it is occasionally useful for the coach to test the athlete when he knows that the athlete will do well. Then the athlete, aware of his progress, will approach competition with confidence.

7. To make the athlete think that he is being coached. This is, perhaps, an unfair use of tests and measurements, but it is an approach which is used by some coaches. This approach will often make a disproportionate impression upon the naïve athlete. The type of situation in which this occurs may involve a coach checking a pulse count and then nodding (or shaking his head) sagely. This may represent an unfair use of the coach's knowledge in order to take advantage of the athlete's ignorance. Not to be done!

Appendix I
Additional Information

Courses

The long standing and widely respected B.A.A.B. Summer School is held annually at Loughborough College. Courses for coaches are of two types:

1. The 'A' course which is an introduction to coaching and covers the full range of events.
2. The 'B' course which is for the more experienced coach and which deals with a group of events and with ancillary aspects of athletics.

The courses are of two weeks duration, although students may be accepted for a one week period.

Teachers and lecturers may claim part of the cost of the course from their local Education Authority.

A course of one week's duration is held annually at the Blackpool Easter course, and approximates to the Loughborough Summer School 'A' course.

Details of the above courses are published some months before the course, and can be seen in the *Times Educational Supplement*.

There are a multitude of other course for coaches, usually of either a day's duration or a week-end duration. These are usually conducted by National Coaches and deal with either an event or a group of events. Details from the Area Coaching Secretary.

There are also a number of courses for young athletes, and it is suggested that coaches encourage young members of their club to attend perhaps one of these each year. Details from the Area Coaching Secretary or the Area National Coach.

Equipment

The coach will probably need:

A tape measure. Whilst the steel tape is the most accurate, it is likely to rust and is easily damaged. For general use it is recommended that the coach buys a nylon tape. For club competition the club should buy (and guard carefully) a longer steel tape.

A stop watch. There are a number of acceptable stop watches on the market. The coach will probably be satisfied with a reasonably robust watch in the £5 – £10 range.

The occasional use of a camera. Almost always there will be a club member or friend who is prepared to film at cost. Still shots are of value, particularly sequence still shots. Of greater value to the coach, however, would be a 'Polaroid' camera. This is a camera which develops the film immediately. Within 10 seconds the coach can pull the developed film out of the back of the camera and comment upon it to the athlete.

Arrangements can occasionally be made to use video tape facilities as an aid to the correction of technical faults. Initial contacts are best made through the Physical Education Department of the nearest University, Polytechnic or College of Education.

The rich coach can also film and project his own movies, 8 mm. being much cheaper than 16 mm.

The track suit should be reasonably up to date. Bri-nylon etc. is in general use at the moment, and may be obtained from a number of firms.

Training shoes are now worn rather than plimsolls.

Spiked shoes will rarely be needed by the coach, but he will need to make recommendations to the athlete with whom he works. Spiked shoes should be tight fitting. The athlete would normally purchase the shoes a size too small and then stretch the shoes to the shape of the feet. This would initially be done by wearing them whilst sitting in front of a fire: then by easy jogging on grass. They should obviously be purchased well in advance of competition. Athletes will normally keep a better pair for competition and use an older pair for training.

Useful Addresses

B.A.A.B. Publications: H. J. Hitchcock, 5 Church Road, Great Bookham, Surrey.
I.A.A.F., 7 Great Winchester Street, London E.C.2.

Some recommended reading

VARIOUS AUTHORS, *B.A.A.B. Instructional Booklets*—available from B.A.A.B. Publications (above).

These booklets each deal with either one or two events and with Strength Training. They have been written by B.A.A.B. coaches. They are written primarily for the young athlete, but can also be of considerable value to the coach. They explain technique, rules and training methods.
Other B.A.A.B. publications may be obtained from the same source. They deal with a number of subjects including judging, athletic injuries, starting and timekeeping. The coach will select according to his interests. Every two or three years the coach should buy the current B.A.A.B. Handbook.

DYSON, G. H. G., *The Mechanics of Athletics* (University of London Press).

An excellent guide to the understanding of the technical aspects of the sport. The coach can glean much from this book, but must not become obsessed with it.

KNAPP, B., *Skill in Sport* (Routledge and Kegan Paul).

Coupled with Dyson's book, this provides fine background reading for the coach who is academically minded.

MCNAB, T. (Ed.), *Modern School Athletics* (University of London Press).

A simple and sound book of value to the teacher and to the young athlete. It also contains a basic and useful section on Tests and Measurements.

CAMPBELL, W. R., and TUCKER, N. M., *An Introduction to Tests and Measurements in Physical Education* (G. Bell).

Appendix II

(a) Jumping 'Decathlon' Tables

The following tables were compiled graphically and extend to cover lower ability ranges. Approximations were made in some cases to prevent fractions of an inch coming in to the scale. In all events except the five stride long jump the mean was taken from test results obtained from non-specialist groups at Young Athlete Courses. In most cases the top mark is that of the approximate world record for the event mainly set by the professional jumpers of the late eighteen hundreds. The mean for the five stride long jump is taken from tests given to specialist jumpers. Hence the tables cannot be used to compare one leaping even with another. Their main aim is to encourage leaping and bounding as an enjoyable means of training for other events with a little direct and indirect competition as an added incentive. The events are not necessarily listed in the best order.

Standing Broad Jump

Both feet together, arms can be used to aid lift. Measurement to nearest point of contact.

Standing Triple

Take off foot to remain in flat contact with the ground although free swinging of non contact leg can be used. The same rule applies to the other three hop, step and jump combinations.

Two hops, Two steps, Two Jumps

The second of the two jumps is made from a two foot take off.

Five Spring Jumps

Five successive two foot-bounds. The feet must be kept together and the movement must be continuous.

Standing four hops and jump

Start as for standing triple. Tables compiled for dominant leg.

Running four hops and jump

Length of run unlimited.

25 yds hop

From standing position. Tables compiled for dominant leg although the mean of left/right should be the recorded performance.

Five stride Long Jump

Normal long jumping rules except that the run is limited to five strides.

Most of the events are educable and improve with training. All ten events allowing two or three successful attempts at each is a good single training session for any power-thirsty athlete.

Tables reproduced by permission of ATHLETICS COACH, published by the British Amateur Athletics Board.

APPENDIX II
JUMPING 'DECATHLON' TABLES
By Wilf Paish

	1 Stand Long Jump	2 Stand Triple Jump	3 2 Hops Step & Jump	4 2 Hops 2 Steps & Jump	5 2 Hops 2 Steps 2 Jumps	6 5 Spring Jumps	7 Stand 4 Hops & Jump	8 Run 4 Hops & Jump	9 25 yds Hop Dom Leg	10 5 Stride Long Jump
100	12' 3"	34' 6"	42' 8"	51' 0"	62' 10"	56' 0"	58' 0"	78' 0"	2.5	23' 11"
99	12' 0"	34' 3"	42' 4"	50' 9"	62' 4"	55' 6"	57' 6"	77' 6"		
98	12' 0"	34' 0"	42' 0"	50' 6"	61' 10"	55' 0"	57' 0"	77' 0"		
97	11' 9"	33' 9"	41' 8"	50' 3"	61' 4"	54' 6"	56' 6"	76' 6"	2.6	23' 10"
96	11' 9"	33' 6"	41' 4"	49' 6"	60' 10"	54' 0"	56' 6"	76' 0"		
95	11' 6"	33' 3"	41' 0"	49' 3"	60' 4"	53' 10"	55' 8"	75' 6"		
94	11' 6"	33' 0"	40' 8"	48' 10"	59' 10"	53' 4"	55' 4"	75' 0"	2.7	
93	11' 3"	32' 9"	40' 4"	48' 6"	59' 4"	53' 0"	55' 0"	74' 6"		
92	11' 3"	32' 6"	40' 0"	48' 2"	58' 10"	52' 6"	54' 6"	74' 0"	2.8	23' 9"
91	11' 0"	32' 3"	39' 8"	47' 10"	58' 4"	52' 0"	54' 0"	73' 4"		23' 8"
90	11' 0"	32' 0"	39' 4"	47' 6"	57' 10"	51' 10"	53' 8"	72' 2"	2.9	
89	10' 9"	31' 9"	39' 0"	47' 2"	57' 4"	51' 4"	53' 4"	71' 6"		
88	10' 9"	31' 6"	38' 8"	46' 10"	56' 10"	51' 0"	53' 0"	71' 0"	3.0	
87	10' 6"	31' 3"	38' 4"	46' 6"	56' 4"	50' 6"	52' 6"	70' 6"	3.1	23' 7"
86	10' 6"	31' 0"	38' 0"	46' 2"	55' 10"	50' 0"	52' 0"	70' 0"		23' 6"
85	10' 3"	30' 9"	37' 8"	45' 10"	55' 6"	49' 10"	51' 8"	69' 6"	3.2	23' 5"
84	10' 3"	30' 6"	37' 4"	45' 6"	55' 0"	49' 4"	51' 4"	69' 0"	3.3	
83	10' 0"	30' 3"	37' 0"	45' 2"	54' 8"	49' 0"	51' 0"	68' 3"	3.4	23' 4"
82	10' 0"	30' 0"	36' 8"	44' 10"	54' 2"	48' 8"	50' 8"	67' 9"	3.5	23' 3"
81	9' 9"	29' 9"	36' 4"	44' 6"	53' 8"	48' 2"	50' 4"	67' 0"	3.6	
80	9' 9"	29' 6"	36' 0"	44' 2"	53' 2"	47' 10"	50' 0"	66' 6"	3.7	
79	9' 6"	29' 3"	35' 8"	43' 10"	52' 10"	47' 4"	49' 6"	66' 0"	3.8	
78	9' 6"	29' 0"	35' 4"	43' 6"	52' 6"	47' 0"	49' 0"	65' 6"	3.9	23' 2"
77	9' 3"	28' 9"	35' 0"	43' 2"	52' 0"	46' 8"	48' 8"	65' 0"	4.0	23' 1"
76	9' 3"	28' 6"	34' 8"	42' 10"	51' 6"	46' 2"	48' 4"	64' 3"	4.1	23' 0"
75	9' 0"	28' 3"	34' 4"	42' 6"	51' 0"	45' 10"	48' 0"	63' 9"	4.2	

APPENDIX II
JUMPING 'DECATHLON' TABLES
By Wilf Paish

	1 Stand Long Jump	2 Stand Triple Jump	3 2 Hops Step & Jump	4 2 Hops 2 Steps & Jump	5 2 Hops 2 Steps 2 Jumps	6 5 Spring Jumps	7 Stand 4 Hops & Jump	8 Run 4 Hops & Jump	9 25 yds Hop Dom Leg	10 5 Stride Long Jump
74	9' 0"	28' 0"	34' 0"	42' 2"	50' 6"	45' 6"	47' 6"	63' 0"	4.3	22' 10"
73	8' 10"	27' 9"	33' 8"	41' 10"	50' 0"	45' 0"	47' 0"	62' 6"	4.4	22' 8"
72	8' 9"	27' 6"	33' 8"	41' 6"	49' 8"	44' 8"	46' 8"	62' 0"	4.5	22' 6"
71	8' 8"	27' 3"	33' 0"	41' 0"	49' 4"	44' 4"	46' 4"	61' 6"	4.6	22' 4"
70	8' 7"	27' 0"	32' 8"	40' 9"	48' 10"	44' 0"	46' 0"	61' 0"	4.7	22' 2"
69	8' 6"	26' 9"	32' 4"	40' 6"	48' 4"	43' 6"	45' 6"	60' 6"	4.8	22' 0"
68	8' 5"	26' 6"	32' 0"	40' 0"	48' 0"	43' 0"	45' 0"	60' 0"	4.9	21' 9"
67	8' 4"	26' 3"	31' 8"	39' 8"	47' 6"	42' 8"	44' 8"	59' 6"	5.0	21' 6"
66	8' 3"	26' 0"	31' 4"	39' 4"	47' 0"	42' 4"	44' 4"	59' 0"	5.1	21' 3"
65	8' 2"	25' 9"	31' 0"	39' 0"	46' 6"	42' 0"	44' 0"	58' 6"	5.2	21' 0"
64	8' 1"	25' 6"	30' 8"	38' 8"	46' 2"	41' 8"	43' 8"	58' 0"	5.3	20' 9"
63	7' 11"	25' 3"	30' 4"	38' 4"	45' 10"	41' 4"	43' 4"	57' 6"	5.4	20' 6"
62	7' 10"	25' 0"	30' 0"	38' 0"	45' 4"	41' 0"	43' 0"	57' 0"	5.5	20' 3"
61	7' 9"	24' 9"	29' 8"	37' 8"	45' 0"	40' 6"	42' 6"	56' 6"	5.6	20' 0"
60	7' 8"	24' 6"	29' 4"	37' 4"	44' 6"	40' 0"	42' 0"	56. 0"	5.7	19' 9"
59	7' 7"	24' 3"	29' 0"	37' 0"	44' 0"	39' 6"	41' 6"	55' 6"	5.8	19' 6"
58	7' 6"	24' 0"	28' 8"	36' 8"	43' 6"	39' 0"	41' 0"	55' 0"	5.9	19' 3"
57	7' 5"	23' 9"	28' 4"	36' 4"	43' 0"	38' 8"	40' 8"	54' 3"	6.0	19' 0"
56	7' 4"	23' 6"	28' 0"	36' 0"	42' 6"	38' 4"	40' 4"	53' 9"	6.1	18' 9"
55	7' 3"	23' 3"	27' 9"	35' 8"	42' 0"	38' 0"	40' 0"	53' 0"	6.2	18' 6"
54	7' 2"	23' 0"	27' 6"	35' 4"	41' 6"	37' 8"	39' 8"	52' 6"	6.3	18' 3"
53	7' 1"	22' 9"	27' 3"	35' 0"	41' 0"	37' 4"	39' 4"	52' 0"	6.4	18' 0"
52	7' 0"	22' 6"	27' 0"	34' 8"	40' 6"	37' 0"	39' 0"	51' 6"	6.5	17' 9"
51	7' 0"	22' 3"	27' 0"	34' 4"	40' 0"	36' 8"	38' 0"	51' 0"	6.6	17' 6"
50	6' 11"	22' 0"	26' 9"	34' 0"	39' 6"	36' 4"	37' 6"	50' 6"	6.7	17' 3"
49	6' 10"	21' 9"	26' 3"	33' 8"	39' 0"	36' 0"	36' 8"	49' 6"	6.8	17' 0"

APPENDIX II
JUMPING 'DECATHLON' TABLES
By WILF PAISH

	1 Stand Long Jump	2 Stand Triple Jump	3 2 Hops Step & Jump	4 2 Hops 2 Steps & Jump	5 2 Hops 2 Steps 2 Jumps	6 5 Spring Jumps	7 Stand 4 Hops & Jump	8 Run 4 Hops & Jump	9 25 yds Hop Dom Leg	10 5 Stride Long Jump
48	6' 9"	21' 6"	26' 0"	33' 4"	38' 6"	35' 8"	36' 4"	49' 0"		16' 10"
47	6' 8"	21' 3"	25' 9"	33' 0"	38' 0"	35' 4"	36' 0"	48' 6"		16' 8"
46	6' 7"	21' 0"	25' 6"	32' 8"	37' 6"	35' 0"	35' 6"	48' 0"		16' 6"
45	6' 6"	20' 9"	25' 3"	32' 4"	37' 0"	34' 8"	35' 0"	47' 6"		16' 4"
44	6' 5"	20' 6"	25' 0"	32' 0"	36' 8"	34' 4"	34' 6"	47' 0"	6.9	16' 2"
43	6' 4"	20' 3"	24' 9"	31' 8"	36' 4"	34' 0"	34' 0"	46' 6"		16' 0"
42	6' 3"	20' 0"	24' 6"	31' 4"	36' 0"	33' 8"	33' 6"	46' 0"	7.0	15' 10"
41	6' 2"	19' 9"	24' 3"	31' 0"	35' 8"	33' 4"	33' 0"	45' 6"		15' 8"
40	6' 1"	19' 6"	24' 0"	30' 8"	35' 4"	33' 0"	32' 6"	45' 0"	7.1	15' 6"
39	6' 0"	19' 3"	23' 9"	30' 4"	35' 0"	32' 8"	32' 0"	44' 6"		15' 4"
38	5' 11"	19' 0"	23' 6"	30' 0"	34' 8"	32' 4"	31' 6"	44' 0"		15' 2"
37	5' 10"	18' 9"	23' 3"	29' 8"	34' 4"	32' 0"	31' 0"	43' 6"	7.2	15' 0"
36	5' 9"	18' 6"	23' 0"	29' 4"	34' 0"	31' 8"	30' 8"	43' 0"	7.3	14' 10"
35	5' 8"	18' 3"	22' 9"	29' 0"	33' 8"	31' 4"	30' 4"	42' 6"		14' 8"
34	5' 7"	18' 0"	22' 6"	28' 8"	33' 4"	31' 0"	30' 0"	42' 0"		14' 6"
33	5' 6"	17' 9"	22' 3"	28' 4"	33' 0"	30' 8"	29' 8"	41' 6"	7.4	14' 4"
32	5' 5"	17' 6"	22' 0"	28' 0"	32' 8"	30' 4"	29' 4"	41' 0"		14' 2"
31	5' 4"	17' 3"	21' 9"	27' 8"	32' 4"	30' 0"	29' 0"	40' 6"	7.5	14' 0"
30	5' 3"	17' 0"	21' 6"	27' 4"	32' 0"	29' 8"	28' 8"	40' 0"	7.5	13' 10"
29	5' 2"	16' 9"	21' 3"	27' 0"	31' 8"	29' 4"	28' 4"	39' 6"	7.6	13' 8"
28	5' 1"	16' 6"	21' 0"	26' 8"	31' 4"	29' 0"	28' 0"	39' 0"		13' 6"
27	5' 0"	16' 3"	20' 9"	26' 4"	31' 0"	28' 8"	27' 8"	38' 6"	7.7	13' 4"
26	4' 11"	16' 0"	20' 6"	26' 0"	30' 8"	28' 4"	27' 4"	38' 0"	7.8	13' 2"
25	4' 10"	15' 9"	20' 3"	25' 8"	30' 4"	28' 0"	27' 0"	37' 6"	7.9	13' 0"
24	4' 9"	15' 6"	20' 0"	25' 4"	30' 0"	27' 8"	26' 8"	37' 0"	8.0	12' 10"

APPENDIX II

JUMPING 'DECATHLON' TABLES

By Wilf Paish

Points	1 Stand Long Jump	2 Stand Triple Jump	3 2 Hops Step & Jump	4 2 Hops 2 Steps & Jump	5 2 Hops 2 Steps 2 Jumps	6 5 Spring Jumps	7 Stand 4 Hops & Jump	8 Run 4 Hops & Jump	9 25 yds Hop Dom Leg	10 5 Stride Long Jump
23	4' 8"	15' 3"	19' 8"	25' 0"	29' 8"	27' 4"	26' 4"	36' 6"		12' 8"
22	4' 7"	15' 0"	19' 4"	24' 8"	29' 4"	27' 0"	26' 0"	36' 0"		12' 6"
21	4' 6"	14' 9"	19' 0"	24' 4"	29' 0"	26' 8"	25' 8"	35' 6"	8.1	12' 4"
20	4' 5"	14' 6"	18' 8"	24' 0"	28' 8"	26' 4"	25' 4"	35' 0"		12' 2"
19	4' 3"	14' 0"	18' 4"	23' 8"	28' 4"	26' 0"	25' 0"	34' 6"		12' 0"
18	4' 2"	13' 9"	18' 0"	23' 4"	28' 0"	25' 8"	24' 8"	34' 0"	8.2	11' 10"
17	4' 1"	13' 6"	17' 8"	23' 0"	27' 8"	25' 4"	24' 4"	33' 6"		11' 8"
16	4' 0"	13' 3"	17' 4"	22' 8"	27' 4"	25' 0"	24' 0"	33' 0"		11' 6"
15	3' 11"	13' 0"	17' 0"	22' 4"	27' 0"	24' 8"	23' 8"	32' 6"	8.3	11' 4"
14	3' 10"	12' 9"	16' 8"	22' 0"	26' 8"	24' 4"	23' 4"	32' 0"		11' 2"
13	3' 9"	12' 6"	16' 4"	21' 8"	26' 4"	24' 0"	23' 0"	31' 6"	8.4	11' 0"
12	3' 8"	12' 3"	16' 0"	21' 4"	26' 0"	23' 8"	22' 8"	31' 0"		10' 8"
11	3' 7"	12' 0"	15' 8"	21' 0"	25' 8"	23' 4"	22' 4"	30' 6"	8.5	10' 4"
10	3' 6"	11' 9"	15' 4"	20' 8"	25' 4"	23' 0"	22' 0"	30' 0"		10' 0"
9	3' 5"	11' 6"	15' 0"	20' 4"	25' 0"	22' 8"	21' 8"	29' 6"	8.5	9' 8"
8	3' 4"	11' 3"	14' 8"	20' 0"	24' 8"	22' 4"	21' 4"	29' 0"		9' 8"
7	3' 3"	11' 0"	14' 4"	19' 8"	24' 4"	22' 0"	21' 0"	28' 6"	8.6	9' 0"
6	3' 2"	10' 6"	14' 0"	19' 4"	24' 0"	21' 8"	20' 8"	28' 0"		8' 8"
5	3' 1"	10' 3"	13' 8"	19' 0"	23' 8"	21' 4"	20' 4"	27' 6"		8' 4"
4	3' 0"	10' 0"	13' 4"	18' 8"	23' 4"	21' 0"	20' 0"	27' 0"	8.7	8' 0"
3	2' 11"	9' 9"	13' 0"	18' 4"	23' 0"	20' 8"	19' 8"	26' 6"		7' 8"
2	2' 10"	9' 6"	12' 8"	18' 0"	22' 8"	20' 4"	19' 4"	26' 0"	8.8	7' 4"
1	2' 0"		12' 4"	17' 8"	22' 0"	20' 0"	19' 0"	25' 6"		7' 0"

(b) Lay-outs for 2000 and 1500 metre Steeple-chase Courses

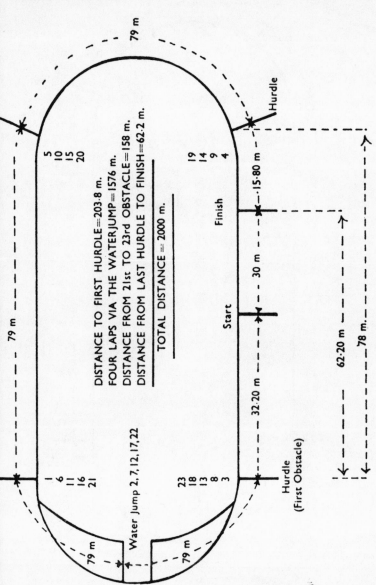

DISTANCE TO FIRST HURDLE = 203·8 m.
FOUR LAPS VIA THE WATERJUMP = 1576 m.
DISTANCE FROM 21st TO 23rd OBSTACLE = 158 m.
DISTANCE FROM LAST HURDLE TO FINISH = 62·2 m.

TOTAL DISTANCE = 2000 m.

FIG. 42. 2000 METRES HURDLES

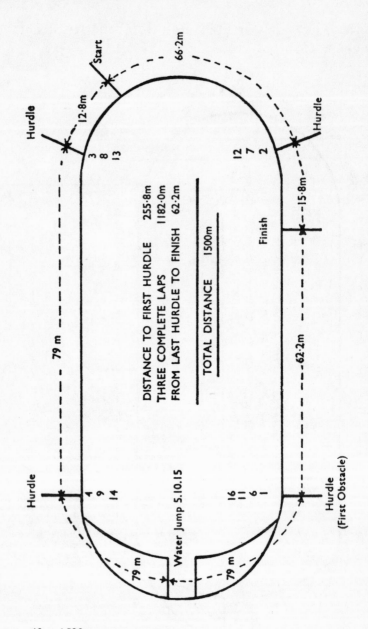

Start

12·8m

66·2m

Hurdle

Hurdle

3
8
13

12
7
2

15·8m

Finish

79 m

DISTANCE TO FIRST HURDLE   255·8m
THREE COMPLETE LAPS   1182·0m
FROM LAST HURDLE TO FINISH   62·2m

TOTAL DISTANCE   1500m

62·2m

Hurdle

4
9
14

Water Jump 5.10.15

16
11
6
1

Hurdle
(First Obstacle)

79 m

79 m

FIG. 43.   1500 METRES HURDLES